The
Sacred
Valley

A guide for leaders with a
deep, bold, consequential faith

PEGGY HAHN

2nd Edition

2017 LEAD

Unless otherwise indicated, all scripture quotations are from the New Revised Standard Version Bible (NRSV), copyright © 1989 by the Division of Christian Education of the National Council of the Churches of Christ in the U.S.A.

Photos were taken by Peggy Hahn and Ashley Dellagiacoma during their travels in Peru.

Artwork by Vonda Drees.

For more information or for bulk orders, contact:
lead@waytolead.org

waytolead.org

ISBN: 978-1506095134

What others are saying about *The Sacred Valley* :

A good discussion of practical aspects of church leadership types and indications of how to approach invigorating congregations to better achieve their missions. This material is backed by extensive, current research of where many congregations are today and how they are being affected by the society changing around them. We are in this for the long haul: our congregations need to provide faith forming cultures to equip people to live their faith as part of all aspects of their lives. I think Peggy provides useful insight on what this demands of church leadership and how to evaluate next steps to get there.

Hahn's insight and metaphor of the journey is wonderful. The artwork is gorgeous and inspiring. A great read for any pastor or layperson discerning where God is leading the church in the future. A must read!

Peggy Hahn is an excellent writer. Her book is a well written, challenging look at what ails many churches today...the lack of leaders that are deep, bold and consequential and not afraid to self assess religious traditions that may be getting in the way of what God is asking us to do in today's rapidly changing world. After all, as she so aptly highlights, it is not our church, but rather God's church and mission. The book builds off her LEAD (Living Every Day as Disciples) studies and uses her trek to Machu Picchu as a framework to introduce new concepts and ideas. I found the book inviting me to join her on a journey of change for our church built on faith in a loving God. Well worth the read.

CONTENTS

CONTENTS

The Leadership Landscape:
What is your rhythm

Four Growth Indicators and Growing Congregations:
Living with purpose

Four Growth Indicators and Out of Breath Congregations:
Learning to lead

The focus of Christian leadership is to grow deep, bold, consequential faith.

This conversation introduces the quadrants on the Leadership Landscape.

The sacred valley calls for leaders who are on a pilgrimage, living with purpose as they listen to God.

This conversation offers insight into the four Growth Indicators and Growing congregations.

The sacred valley can wear leaders out as they hit roadblocks of conflict, decline, uncertainty or a lack of confidence on the pilgrimage.

This conversation considers the challenges for Out of Breath congregations and the four Growth Indicators.

CONTENTS

Four Growth Indicators and Stalled Congregations:
Done learning

Four Growth Indicators and Becoming Congregations:
Leading to live

Follow to Lead:
Living every day as disciples

The sacred valley can narrow our perspective, driving people to look to the past at what is known rather than looking to a future that is largely unknown.

This conversation reflects on the reality for Stalled congregations and the four Growth Indicators.

The sacred valley is an invitation to new beginnings, to new and renewed leadership.

This conversation takes up the gifts and challenges of new and Becoming congregations and the four Growth Indicators.

And now faith, hope and love abide, these three; and the greatest of these is love. - *1 Corinthians 13:13*

This conversation offers a systems perspective with a snapshot of the Congregational Assessment, a path for a new movement of leaders, and case studies.

CONTENTS

9

To share the sacred valley experience, you have to tell the story.

This conversation introduces lag and lead metrics in a congregational setting.

LEAD is deeply grateful for the many other researchers, writers, poets, artists, and mentors that continue to lead the way as we discover what God is doing in a changing world.

This section includes terms, books, and people that are referenced throughout *The Sacred Valley*.

Learn from yesterday, live for today, hope for tomorrow.

The important thing is not to stop questioning.
- *Albert Einstein*

Life is a pilgrimage where the journey is every
bit as important as the destination.

This book is dedicated to all those who hear
the call of Christian leadership and respond
by growing themselves and others.

Foreword to 2nd Edition

I serve as the Pastor of a congregation that has been through – and continues to travel along – a journey of renewal. I know well the work that ministry leaders put into finding the right resources to grow as leaders and to help the ministries they serve to live into their calling and mission. I know well the frustrations that come with seeking to reignite the passion and purpose of a community.

The congregation I serve – Spirit of Joy! Lutheran Church – is not unique in the Lutheran church or in the broader landscape of religious life in America at the beginning of the 21st Century. Over the course of twenty years, we experienced diminishing attendance, contributions, and enthusiasm. There was no one factor to blame; momentum just continued to push us in the same direction. We were dwindling toward irrelevance. Sound familiar?

Our leaders saw a choice. Were we going to close or were we going to survive?

We decided on a third choice: we were not going to close, we were not going to survive, we were going to thrive – because that is who we believe God is calling us to be as we proclaim Jesus' good news.

Which was great! We decided that we were going to thrive... but how would we go about doing that?

Countless ministries find themselves at that place.

Let me give you a shortcut to what I discovered in our ministry: LEAD has talked to leaders who have walked through these same choices. The LEAD team spent time listening to leaders who were exhausted and ministries that were energized. LEAD talked to the leaders of ministries that chose to faithfully close, others that continued to struggle to survive, and those that chose to live into God's vision of thriving ministry.

And after hundreds of conversations, learning from innumerable leaders, the LEAD team distilled what they learned into this book in your hand and released it to the church two years ago.

I came to be a part of the LEAD team because the things that they learned – the things we have continued to learn – actually work. I've seen it firsthand. The congregation I serve is thriving – we have moved from being an Out of Breath congregation to a Becoming congregation. And in that process, the members of our community have become more passionate about their faith, about our mission together, and about the neighborhood we serve.

In the two years since the first edition of The Sacred Valley was released, the LEAD team has continued to learn. We have integrated insights from congregations that have used our resources, from continued conversations with leaders from across the church, and from the neighborhoods that those ministries are a part of.

Let me be clear: In this book, you will not find another program – there are no "10 Steps to Save Your Church" (and if that's what you are looking for, you can stop – Jesus already saved all of us, including our churches).

Instead, you will find a way to reframe your ministry – a frame that helps you to see those places where God is revealing your ministry's unique purpose.

After all of our conversations, all of our learning, all of the leaders who have taught us about their ministry, this is what we have seen work – and we believe it can work for you.

Dear leader, God has called you to an amazing journey. In a world that is changing ever-more rapidly, leaders with deep, bold, consequential faith are needed now more than ever to shepherd the work of God's kingdom in our local neighborhoods.

And wherever you are on the pilgrimage of leadership – we offer this book as a resource and guide for your journey.

It will not be an easy, simple, or quick journey.

But it most certainly is joyful, rewarding, and deeply meaningful.

So come and join the conversation with us.

Pastor David Hansen

First and foremost, David is a congregational pastor. This is his passion and the calling he gives his time and energy to. David believes that church is more than congregation and that when we can help each other to share the Good News and grow God's Kingdom, we should. This conviction has brought David around the country helping congregations and organizations to communicate more effectively and pass the faith on from generation to generation. As a volunteer, David has been on the communications team of the Gulf Coast Synod for many years. He has also served on the five-person Social Media Team of the 2015 ELCA Youth Gathering and is part of the leadership team for the Church Social Media community helping the church to use digital tools to share the Good News.

Foreword to 1st Edition

Has there ever been a time when leadership was more needed in our congregations and world, yet in such short supply?

In his book *Accelerate*, John Kotter, professor emeritus at Harvard University and well known author of books on change and leadership, writes, "The world is now changing at a rate at which the basic systems, structures, and cultures built over the past century cannot keep up with the demands being placed on them. Incremental adjustments to how you manage and strategize, no matter how clever, are not up to the job. You need something very new to stay ahead in an age of tumultuous change and growing uncertainties." (page vii)

He goes on to contrast the role of *management*—planning, budgeting, organizing, staffing, problem-solving—with the role of *leadership*—establishing direction, aligning people, motivating people, inspiring, mobilizing people to achieve astonishing results, and most importantly *propelling us into the future*. While an organization needs both roles, in this era of "tumultuous change and growing uncertainties" we need visionary, credible, values-driven, skilled leaders who are willing to lead by example.

LEAD is all about fostering leadership for this fast changing world. It is about developing Christian leaders who will be the catalysts for growing a deep, bold, consequential faith in Jesus Christ in all ages and generations. It is about developing Christian leaders who are deepening their faith in Jesus Christ, who are cultivating a spirituality for the long haul, and who are alert to the signs of God at work in our church and world.

To grow a deep, bold, consequential faith in Jesus Christ in all ages and generations, Christian leaders need to develop congregations that are faith forming cultures—providing a crucible for the formation of a Christian way of life and equipping people to live their faith at home and in the world. So LEAD is also all about congregational renewal because the faith and life of the congregation makes a huge difference in developing children, youth, adults, and families of committed Christian faith.

In the research that led to *the Spirit and Culture of Youth Ministry* book (Martinson, Black, and Roberto) we discovered (again) the power of faith forming congregational cultures. In the exemplary congregations we studied, we found youth and parents who had come to know a living and active God through their relationships with God and the community. The young people in these congregations got to know Jesus Christ through the witness of believers and ongoing relationships with persons and communities who know Jesus. We found that the power of faithful, multi-generational Christian relationships are at the heart of a congregational culture that develops and nurtures Christian faith in all ages and generations.

These faith forming congregational cultures possess a sense of God's living presence in community, worship, study, and service. They make faith and discipleship central—teaching people how to be a Christian, how to discover the meaning of the Bible for their lives, how to pray, and how to serve others. They make mission central—consistently witnessing, serving, promoting moral responsibility, and seeking justice. They are welcoming, inclusive, and hospitable communities for all people—placing an emphasis on providing love, support, and friendship. They worship God through spiritually uplifting worship experiences that are enlightening, inspiring, and relevant in daily life.

So why is LEAD so important today? First, LEAD is about us as leaders—helping us reflect, discern, and pray about our call and responsibility to be Christian leaders in the 21st century. Take time to reflect on the words and images in this book and weave them into your prayer life.

Second, LEAD is about the future of our congregations—providing us with the vision, practices, tools, and resources to bring the vision of vital and vibrant faith forming communities to life in the 21st century. Is there any work more important for us as Christian leaders?

In closing I am reminded of this beautiful verse from Psalm 119, "Your word is a lamp to my feet and a light to my path" (v. 105). LEAD can be a light to us on our path as Christian leaders as we seek to develop a deep, bold, consequential faith in the lives of all ages and generations in our communities.

John Roberto

John Roberto has been and continues to be an innovator in Catholic Religious Education and Youth Ministry. John is best known for his practical application of the vision and theory for ministry with and for people of all ages and stages in their lifelong growth in faith. He has a particular expertise in formation praxis for youth in the teenage years. John works as a consultant to churches and national organizations, teaches courses, and conducts workshops in faith formation. He has authored many books and program manuals including 21st Century Faith Formation and curates the Lifelong Learning digital resource center at lifelonglearning.org.

Introduction

A guide for leaders with a deep, bold, consequential faith

Jesus gave us a vision for Christian leadership:
Live every day as a disciple

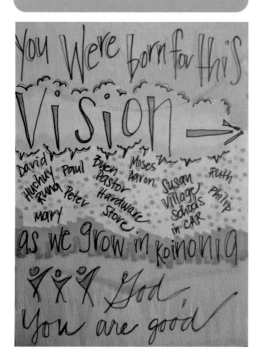

You were born for this.

This is our watch. Like it or not, you and I are called to lead the Christian movement forward each in our own unique way even as we are struggling to find the path ourselves. We can't focus on everything so we are compelled to set priorities. In this book, you will discover four primary behaviors that effectively shift your mindset as a leader and prepare your faith communities for leadership in a changing world. Through LEAD's research into the differences between growing and stalled congregations, these four behaviors stand out as clear indicators for growth. They exist in thriving Christian communities around the world; I have personally witnessed these growth indicators at work in communities of all sizes and geographies in the United States, El Salvador, Peru, and the Central African Republic. We can do this!

We are all part of a long line of faithful servants who were often as unsure of themselves as we are. Yet today we find their stories in the Bible and turn to them for support. Think about Abram and Sarai, Moses, Elizabeth and Mary; you get the drift. It may feel audacious to compare ourselves to these saints of the faith yet LEAD is convinced that on their watch, they had their own doubts and fears. We can courageously say that when reading scripture, it is these same behaviors—the four Growth Indicators—that appear.

The same God who accompanied these amazing leaders is walking with us right now. In some small way, our lives are part of this story.

The Sacred Valley answers the question, "What does it mean to grow leaders with a deep, bold, consequential faith during the greatest cultural shifts that have ever taken place in our world?" It is not the last word or even the first word, but it is a guide for Christian leaders who are looking for a path forward. LEAD is committed to training and resourcing these leaders who train and lead others.

This book, in its second edition, is an overview of LEAD's best thinking. In addition there are four companion books with processes to help leaders put these concepts into practice. Examples of congregations who have done so are shared in Chapter 8, *Follow to LEAD*. This book, like the ministry of LEAD, reflects what it means to love God with all our heart, soul, mind, and strength. The Disciple Frame, described in Chapter 2, provides a framework for integrating the following four ways of loving God and of loving each other.

What LEAD means by:

Deep:
Leaders actively engaging in spiritual practices

Bold:
Leaders having the courage to help others grow

Consequential:
Leaders doing things that matter

HEART: Loving God with all our heart calls us to listen to God's voice with a bias toward action. As we listen, we are moved to do justice in the world, neighborhood, workplace, school, congregation, and family.

Christian leadership is a pilgrimage rather than a destination. Pilgrims understand that meaning is found in the moment, not the milestones. This book includes the invitation to go on your own spiritual pilgrimage.

You are invited into a virtual trip, imagining the Inca Trail with its sacred space, milestones, physical, emotional, and mental challenges as a metaphor for your own personal journey. Join the story of others who have made this trek. Reflect on your own past pilgrimages or make plans for a new one. You don't have to leave the country to experience God moving in everyday life.

The heart moves us to act out of our awareness of God's love. Recognizing that the church is not a building but rather a way of life found in us all is a key paradigm shift. When we wake up to God moving, even the mundane becomes sacred. And when we know we are loved by God, loving others is irresistible. The more we trust in God's love, the more we love.

SOUL: Loving God with all of our soul calls us to center. Waking up to our own identity and opening ourselves to God's love and grace moves us to build purposeful community.

Centering happens when God's people experience a deepening relationship with God and ultimately with one another. Our relationships drive our values and our choices, impacting how we use our time and our resources. This soul work affects our very way of being as we increase our awareness of God's love.

When we work to align our lives around a shared purpose and clear core values, we sense the alignment in our soul. Our identity becomes clearer, even to ourselves. When this happens in a faith community, the congregation becomes transformed. Shared core values including Core Beliefs, Core Convictions, and Core Practices are contagious. These core values strive to answer the question, "Why do we exist?" This kind of focus empowers leaders to stop or start ministries with greater confidence.

MIND: Loving God with all of our mind calls us to explore. Embracing new perspectives, asking questions, and becoming aware of our blind spots opens our mindset about God and life.

God has given us the capacity to ask questions, to rethink assumptions, to take risks, and to innovate. LEAD encourages strategic thinking about our theology, governance, staffing, and our life of generosity.

In this time of change, there is high risk in maintaining the status quo. Congregational inertia has a bias toward pleasing people. The only way forward is to explore the new world emerging around us. Carol Dweck's work on mindsets assures us that people can move from a fixed to a growth mindset.

We are called to lead beyond the current paradigms and to discover what God is doing. We are also called to steward the treasures of our traditions and rituals. This is the very tension that drives us to our knees as we do the hard work of expanding our mindset. How we think about things really matters.

STRENGTH: Loving God with all of our strength calls us to connect. Expanding beyond our comfort zone to embrace a diverse world moves us toward God's desire for wholeness.

Humanity is a beautiful tapestry of unique, God-created beings representing the richness of God's creation, yet the word "diversity" generates a wide range of emotions in people including fear, anger, hate, love, or hope. LEAD uses diversity in the fullest sense of that word. Most of us have not embraced true community as God intended it. We can do better! Connecting to each other at a deeper level, especially with people different from ourselves, includes moving past superficial relationships, stereotypes, and assumptions.

We are stronger when our relational connections include an ever-increasing move toward diversity. Working out of our comfort zone expands our self-awareness and our God-awareness.

It is easy to think we know people without moving to deeper intimacy. Congregations are unintentionally designed to keep relationships shallow. The very culture of congregational life can work against authenticity and integrity—two values that are essential for true community. When leaders are willing to be vulnerable, relating to others with transparency, true relationships and trust can grow. Deepening trust allows us to expand our worldview.

We are loved by the God of relationships. We worship a God who in God's self as God, Christ, and the Holy Spirit is the very essence of relationships, demonstrating for all of us the gift of interdependence. Our connections with people who are different than ourselves strengthens our own identity and way of life. It is only through this work of expanding our connections that we fully embrace God's vision for the world.

O God, full of compassion, we commit and commend ourselves to you, in whom we live and move and have our being. Be the goal of our pilgrimage, and our rest by the way. Give us refuge from the turmoil of worldly distractions beneath the shadow of your wings. Let our hearts, so often a sea of restless waves, find peace in you, O God; through Jesus Christ our Lord. Amen - *Evangelical Lutheran Worship*

¡BUEN CAMINO! (bwane kah-MEEN-oh) Christian leadership is a pilgrimage rather than a destination. Imagine hiking the Inca Trail with its sacred space, milestones, physical, emotional, and mental challenges as a metaphor for your own personal journey. "Buen Camino" or "Good Journey" rings out among the pilgrims on the trail and this same blessing can be shared with leaders as we navigate the path through these changing times following God into the world.

A LEAD Best Practice:
Our information comes from listening

LEAD teaches a process called Tune In which involves intentional listening. LEAD has listened one-on-one to over 800 pastors and even more lay leaders at the time of this writing. The first 60 sessions were held with pastors all within a single three-week period. You would be surprised how clear things become with that kind of intense, focused time with professional leaders. We encourage you to try the Tune In process in your own neighborhood. A step by step guide to the process is available on the LEAD website at waytolead.org/tune-in.

LEAD's research is not finished—it is an ongoing way of life. We will continue to listen to leaders who are asking hard questions and doing their best to grow themselves and to grow their congregations. And through this face-to-face listening we will continue to learn. Themes have emerged and these observations have been validated by the research of others who discovered the same things long before we did.

What we have found is too important to keep to ourselves. In this book, we share the patterns we have found and the conclusions we have drawn about the current leadership landscape. We want to start a conversation so you can see how it resonates with your own experience.

The phrase "Leadership Landscape" has been selected intentionally to refer to an ever-changing environment that varies by season. The Leadership Landscape is a circle divided by two axes into four unique quadrants. Leaders of all types and in all stages of life can place themselves on the Leadership Landscape. More on that in Chapter 3, *The Leadership Landscape*.

Listening has taught us that there are clear behaviors that leaders in each quadrant practice—sometimes intentionally, sometimes not. When leaders make a choice to grow and begin practicing some specific new behaviors, they mature. These behaviors are grouped into four primary categories called the four Growth Indicators. These Growth Indicators are reliable and consistent in producing sustainable behavior change.

LEAD grows leaders who grow other leaders. When "How-Tos" are introduced in this and other LEAD books or resources, they do not provide a list of results. They offer stories of how leaders who have practiced these behaviors have been effective. The intent is not to predetermine how God will use us to impact our world. Different leaders in diverse settings and socio-economic situations with unique cultures, languages, histories, and levels of experience can apply the four Growth Indicators to grow themselves and others in new and exciting ways.

According to the authors of *Influencer*,
Before you can influence change, you have to decide what you are trying to change. Influence geniuses focus on behaviors. They don't dive into developing influence strategies until they've carefully identified the behaviors they want to influence. A few behaviors can drive a lot of change.

The change LEAD is committed to is growing leaders with a deep, bold, consequential faith. The shape this takes will be different across the world, yet the behaviors that produce growth are the same. For LEAD, deep, bold, consequential faith looks like:

⊕ Leaders deepening their faith life by taking the initiative to encounter God in new ways and engaging in spiritual practices

⊕ Leaders boldly learning new skills, accessing tools, and creating networks with courage to grow self and others in faith and leadership

⊕ Leaders doing things that matter with the conviction and confidence to guide faith communities that respond to human need and suffering in the local and global community, living a consequential faith

LEAD is still listening; I am still listening. This book is just the beginning. Join the conversation on Facebook at LEAD: Living every day as disciples.

The best leaders are the best followers. People listen more closely to people who are listening to them. Sensitivity to people's needs and interests is a key ingredient to building trust. - *Kouzes & Posner*

1 Location:

Entering the Sacred Valley

Christian leadership is asking more of us than ever before.

The first gift about Christian leadership that I received from the beautiful Peruvian Andes was this: I am not in as good a shape as I think I am.

By the end of the first day of a four day pilgrimage on the ancient Inca Trail, hikers have to make a choice: either return to Cusco or continue the hike to Machu Picchu. Committing to the journey requires stepping out into an uncertain future. While the ancient Incans literally ran the trail, hikers like me are a very different story.

In terms of physical effort, it seems that walking three hours in my neighborhood equals about five minutes of hiking in the Andes.

No kidding. Between the elevation, up to 14,000 feet which is a big deal for a flat-lander from the Gulf Coast, and the incline, the comparison is laughable. In the Andes, you are either going up or going down; there is no such thing as flat (don't trust the guides who say "Peruvian flat!"), so forward movement becomes as much a head trip as it is a physical act. I quickly learned that success in hiking or leadership is as much about how you think as it is about what you do.

Every leader and every congregation can grow. *

* Some congregations choose not to grow.

Put another way: persevere or panic! We can talk ourselves into trying hard things we have never done before and attempting to move in a new direction or we can just as effectively talk ourselves into a panic and resist something uncertain. What we say to ourselves really matters. We can set a posture of openness or we can close the door to expanding our worldview and God-view by how we behave and think. Growth is a choice we make.

This is about a readiness to become more of ourselves, growing into who God made us to be. A real walk in faith. It is the birthright of every person on the planet to strive to be more fully human. We never age-out of our capacity to grow and learn nor are we ever too young, too old, or too inexperienced to try.

> What we say to ourselves matters.
>
> Growth is a choice we make that influences new behaviors.

You may have already realized, as we did in the Andes, that the landscape we travel today is harder than we ever imagined. We trained in ways we thought would be helpful only to discover we were sadly unprepared for the terrain. God gave gifts to each of us hikers that not only kept us safe on the ancient Inca Trail but also keep us focused on the old, worn path of Christian leadership. Like this hike, we all navigate a changing world that is somewhere between the past and the future. Most of us do not feel equipped for the call we hear, yet we are doing our best to follow

God into the future. As we encounter new technologies and worldviews that challenge, frustrate, and exhaust us, God is there working through us as we struggle and continually surprising us!

Leadership involves influence and we may want to lead others yet be unsure of exactly what or how to do that. Like it or not, most of us discover that we are not in as good a shape as we thought we were. At the moment that we admit this truth, on the Inca Trail or in a leadership situation, we are ready to grow. Growth is a choice made by people or communities motivated to be more effective.

The good news is that God is ahead of us, creating a future we are only beginning to imagine. God's love is as reliable as ever and we can have confidence that the promise made to the first disciples, "...remember, I am with you always, to the end of the age," *Matthew 28:20,* is ours as well.

Welcome to life in the valley

A valley is a low area between hills, often with a river running through it. This is where we are located right now in the Christian movement. We are in this space, the sacred valley, between the ancient past and the not-yet future. Many wonderful writers have offered data, historical perspectives, and theological wisdom that inform our spiritual GPS. The leaders referred to in this book are listed in the *Books Referenced* section at the end. People like Phyllis Tickle have been especially encouraging. She wrote in her book, *The Great Emergence,* that every 500 years when the world and the church go through a social, political, economic, and religious transformation, we can be assured that the Christian movement grows. This is great news. But the problem with being in the sacred valley is that we lack confidence because we cannot see the end of the trail. In times like this, we must do what leaders have always done, have a little faith and pay attention to the bright spots. In their book *Switch,* Heath and Heath point to the idea of following bright spots as an effective method for making change.

There are definitely bright spots! LEAD has discovered certain behaviors that will help us navigate the trail. We encounter them over and over as we study leaders and look at faith communities that are growing. LEAD calls these the **four Growth Indicators: Listen, Center, Explore, and Connect.** Research shows that these behaviors are critical to growth making them a great place to start. Think of the Growth Indicators as trailheads, not the destination. Look for more information on these four Growth Indicators in later chapters.

What is important to know is that these four Growth Indicators are not uniquely Christian. They are at the core of organizations like Weight Watchers and Alcoholics Anonymous (A.A.) with proven track records for changing people's lives by changing behaviors. These programs work when individuals invest their lives in making them work. As you will see in Chapter 4, *Four Growth Indicators and Growing Congregations,* these four Growth Indicators are designed for people living in the valley.

The first step is to choose to change. At Weight Watchers, when you decide to lose weight you are given strategies to reach your goal. If you admit you have a problem with alcohol, A.A.'s Twelve Steps "are a group of principles, spiritual in their nature, which, if practiced as a way of life,

A Search for
Vital Behaviors

If we understand leadership as influence, it turns out that there are specific behaviors that matter more than others. The more precisely we can focus on certain behaviors, the more likely we are to create momentum for the results we hope to accomplish. Start by asking:

"What must people do in order to improve the situation?"

The power to change requires the wisdom to know what behaviors to change.

Scripting the moves of behavior is one of the most effective ways of making change.

can expel the obsession to drink and enable the sufferer to become happily and usefully whole."

Both of these organizations are striving for sustainable behavior change: new, healthier ways of life.

They both expect that:
⊕ People hear stories from others who are struggling and share their own stories. (Listen)
⊕ People shift their mindset with a moment of self-awareness and show up for help. (Center)
⊕ People progress toward sustainable behavior change by learning, using new resources, and working a plan. (Explore)
⊕ People participate in a supportive community that holds one another accountable. (Connect)

A.A. and Weight Watchers do not promise it will be easy. What they provide are real behaviors that help people navigate the valley. A.A. and Weight Watchers are only effective when people apply what they learn and develop life-changing habits. We have much to learn from our brothers and sisters who have walked through these sacred valleys.

Before we begin changing other people or our own congregations, we need to change ourselves. By the power of the Holy Spirit, with real commitment and openness, growth is possible for all of us.

We believe that all people and organizations, including congregations, can grow. Growth is a choice to shift mindsets, learn new behaviors, and deepen faith.

Growth is a choice that is motivated by the Holy Spirit prompting individuals to act. God stirs up individuals and communities through the actions of passionate leaders who have heard a call to serve. These people respond by growing themselves and others for the sake of the Gospel of Jesus Christ. The very act of hearing and responding to God's call allows God's kingdom to break into the world. We are actually hard-wired by God to listen and respond.

Every person has a hunger to exercise personal agency—to contribute, to make a positive difference, to influence, to help, to build—and in this sense, to lead. Even young children want to express their unique and developing gifts by helping others. We are born with this God-given urge to make an impact within our own circle of influence whether that circle is large or small. More than three decades of research documents the impact that parents make in their child's faith. Never underestimate the value of growing leaders of faith, including parents, who will follow God into a changing world.

In *Drive*, Daniel Pink points out that the secret to high performance and satisfaction at work, school, home, and church is in the deeply human need to direct our own lives, to learn and create new things, and to do better by ourselves in our world. It is out of both this basic understanding of how we are wired and our confidence that the Holy Spirit is moving among us that growth is possible. LEAD has been listening deeply to leaders and we offer a framework for understanding the current Leadership Landscape and the four Growth Indicators that will shape the path.

By the grace of God, we are all connected to a global community of believers through a variety of traditions that help us see we are in it together. This is at the heart of our Baptismal Covenant whether we entered into the community as an infant or as an adult. As we hold each other in prayer, we can also be encouraging and challenging each other, providing accountability for growth.

Somewhere along the way we have confused being nice with Christian love; true love calls a thing what it is. Our current behavior could make others think that we have a greater concern for not hurting people's feelings

than we do for waking up each morning as forgiven people trying to live a little more like Jesus.

In the chapters ahead, we will unpack the four Growth Indicators in a Christian context and show how each indicator is a predictor of growth. We will explain how particular behaviors lead to measurable results, creating new metrics for leaders as they grow and as they grow others.

> Even though I walk through the darkest valley, I fear no evil, for you are with me;
> your rod and your staff, they comfort me.
> - *Psalm 23:4*

Just like A.A. or Weight Watchers, these indicators are only helpful if they shape behavior. It is our prayer that you find yourself in this book.

2 The Disciple Frame:

What you see is what you get

Vision is at the heart of leadership.

When you look at this photo, what do you see first, Ashley or the Incan Ruins?

The tension between looking at what is closest to us and what is in the distance is always part of a leader's challenge. Without a frame of reference, leaders can move from one good new idea or program to another without ever really having a vision for the future. Framing what you see and do is the beginning of alignment and perspective.

We all have frames. Many times these are unintentional but they shape our perspective,

maybe even blocking our view. Similar to the impact your mindset has on leadership, the frame through which you look will be a game changer.

My second leadership gift from the Inca Trail was a surprise; I discovered the unexpected impact a frame of reference can have. On the second day out of four, there was a moment when I felt a crushing weight on my chest. It was my Gulf Coast lungs trying to breathe at almost 14,000 feet. I knew in my head that I was past the point where turning around was an option. I'm not saying that I was panicking, but I was keenly aware that the Andes were testing my faith. With every few feet of forward movement, I was stepping aside while a porter ran past me, literally ran, carrying our tents or a stack of chairs and pots and who-knows-what on their backs so they could provide for our every need. It was both impressive and intimidating. Then all of a sudden, as I was gasping for breath, there he was, Oswaldo, one of our guides, walking beside me.

Our conversation went something like this...
Oswaldo: You are doing great.
Me: I can't breathe.
Oswaldo: You need to get a rhythm.
Me: Huh?
Oswaldo: Set a pace of walking and breathing that works for you. Focus on the rhythm.
Me: Ok.

It turns out I could walk for 12 steps before stopping to breathe three times and then walk 12 more steps. It worked. The more I leaned into the rhythm, the more distance I could cover. Once I got the rhythm down, I realized I could pray the Lord's Prayer during the steps and stop to breathe during the pauses. Then I could actually enjoy the beauty of the Andes. It was a rhythm of activity and rest.

I needed a different frame of reference to shift my view from "I can't" to "I can." Once I was operating within this new frame, I could actually envision reaching my goal. It became clear to me—what you see is what you get!

So what is our perspective of Christian leadership?

In the book *In the Name of Jesus*, Henri Nouwen argues

> ...the Christian leader of the future is called to be completely irrelevant and to stand in this world with nothing to offer but his or her own vulnerable self. That is the way Jesus came to reveal God's love.

Jesus's life is our best example of what faithful leadership looks like. His words and the intentional leadership training he gave his disciples as they traveled across the country together are still helpful to us today.

As LEAD sought to define Christian leadership, we realized that Jesus had already done this in Mark 12:29-31, Matthew 22:36-38, and Luke 10:27-29. We call this The Disciple Frame. Jesus's words, and Moses's too, give us a perspective that shapes all we do.

> Jesus answered, "The first is, 'Hear, O Israel: the Lord our God, the Lord is one; you shall love the Lord your God with all your heart, and with all your soul, and with all your mind, and with all your strength.'
> The second is this, 'You shall love your neighbor as yourself. There is no other commandment greater than these.'"
> - Mark 12:29-31

In fact by placing the four Growth Indicators inside The Disciple Frame, they become grounded in the ancient faith practices spoken by Moses and expanded upon by Jesus.

For Hebrew people even today, these words are sacred. They give meaning to life and are known as the Shema (pronounced Shmah). In Jesus's time, each day began and ended with the recitation of the Shema, ancient Israel's concise crystallization of its central convictions. It was taught to Jesus as it was to every Jewish child. Twice a day, in accordance with Jewish practice, Jesus recited, perhaps chanted, these same words.

As an integral part of Jesus's daily life, when he was asked by one of the teachers of the law, "Of all the commandments, which is the most important?" everyone listening already knew his answer. He was reminding them of who they were.

These words have deep meaning for Christians too. It is with the words of the Shema that Jesus answers the question, "What is Christian leadership?"

Notice that in Mark, Chapter 12, Jesus claims the Shema as the First Commandment and adds a second that summarizes the other nine, almost as though it had been there all along, saying, "You shall love your neighbor as yourself." It is clear that right after loving God with all that we have and all that we are, our next move is to love our neighbor and ourselves.

Jesus's words provide the frame that defines and sets the path for Christian leadership. It is different from leadership in the marketplace, on the athletic field, or in the classroom. Leadership in the faith community is unique because the bottom line is growing faith in Jesus and the witness of Jesus Christ in the world. In the end, the greatest commodity of a congregation, and therefore of its leadership, is trusted relationships, not money. Through the power of the Holy Spirit, people of faith are sent to live lives of pilgrimage bearing God's creative and redeeming word to all the world. It is a purposeful value system that grows out of the promises of baptism both freeing us and entrusting us with the responsibility to grow ourselves and others.

> Pilgrimage—a journey or search of moral or spiritual significance The journey may be to a shrine or place of importance to a person's beliefs and faith or a metaphorical journey into one's own beliefs.
>
> Every day can be understood as a pilgrimage.

The image on the next page helps illustrate The Disciple Frame. The four ways of loving God listed in the Shema are each distinct yet interconnected.

The Disciple Frame provides perspective in this time of great change. The ancient call to love God with our whole being is so simple and yet so complicated as we work to put it into practice. Without the frame, it is easy to lose our way and think that our congregation, our programs, our meetings, our budgets, our own "you name its," are what ministry is about.

The Disciple Frame helps us focus just like our Peruvian guide Oswaldo taught us to on the Inca Trail. Our point of view is shaped by what we see. When all we could see were miles and miles of tiny little stone steps going uphill, we missed the fact that we had the privilege of walking on an ancient path that at one time connected the whole Incan empire much like social media connects us today. We missed the beauty of the Andes. We missed listening to God speak to us in the beauty of the moment because we were focused on survival.

What we see is what we get. As long as leaders see decline in their faith community, a shrinking bank account, and fewer young people engaged in ministry, we miss what God is already doing. Our vision of gloom and doom becomes a self-fulfilling prophecy. The Disciple Frame helps us keep a God-size vision in front of us. It reminds us of our own call to love deeply. It helps us take our eyes off of ourselves to see the wider view, God's view, of our world. Living inside The Disciple Frame puts everything in perspective.

The Disciple Frame with the four Growth Indicators

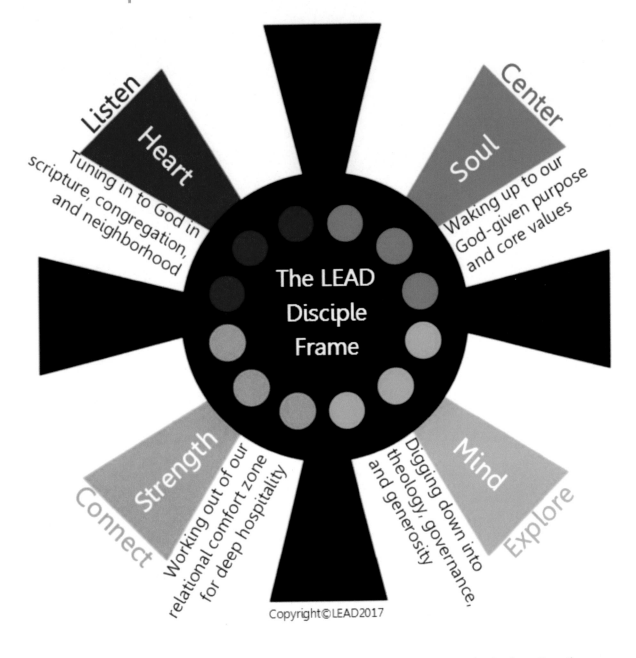

Copyright©LEAD2017

Notice that the four ways of loving God found in the Shema shape what we do in the four Growth Indicators. The Disciple Frame is a way of life with built in behaviors and an ancient set of metrics we can embrace today.

A Thank You Note: LEAD's thinking about the words of Jesus in the Greatest Commandment as a path for Christian leadership and a call to deeper discipleship was inspired by Pastor Rich Nelson. You can learn more about his work at followingtheway.me.

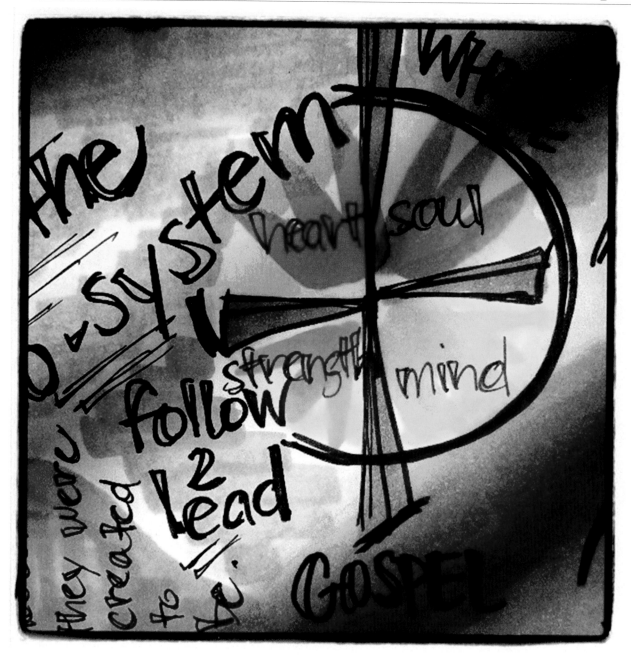

Personal Reflection on The Disciple Frame ~ Peggy

We wrestle with our faith every day—maybe every hour on some days. This idea of loving God is only possible because of the lavish love and unearned grace we receive from God. The Disciple Frame is not meant to be a metric but rather a compass for living out our less than perfect lives as leaders. Each of us has to navigate life with crucial questions. As leaders we must ask ourselves: What values guide our lives as others watch? How do we want to influence others (even our own children or grandchildren)? Leadership is about influence and comes with a responsibility to take our own growth seriously. How will we receive God's love so that we might learn to love God more each day with all of our heart, soul, mind, and strength? What kind of faith leaders do we want to be? In the end, it's all about living every day as disciples.

Living in The Disciple Frame

Loving God with all our heart, soul, mind, and strength offers us clear practices for our lives. LEAD has created ways to move intentionally into one or more of these areas of loving God and begin growing a more deep, bold, consequential faith. There is a relationship between these four practices and a sequence that is helpful for leaders and faith communities. Try a few of these practices:

HEART calls us to listen

The point? To live out of a growing view of God and act out of a larger worldview.

Practices:

⊕ Keep a gratitude journal

⊕ Pray daily for your neighbors

⊕ Listen to others while suspending judgement

⊕ Notice when you falsely assume everyone thinks like you

⊕ Travel outside of your comfort zone

⊕ Ask clarifying questions to learn more about another's worldview

SOUL calls us to center

The point? To deepen our relationship with God and each other with clear values rooted in our faith.

Practices:

⊕ Recognize God moving in your daily life

⊕ Study scripture with a small group

⊕ Spend quiet time in prayer

⊕ Walk a labyrinth or stations of the cross

⊕ Meet with a spiritual guide

⊕ Pray with a friend

⊕ Reflect on your own faith story

STRENGTH calls us to connect

The point? To embrace an ever-growing understanding of God's diversity, respecting the gifts, stories, and values of others.

Practices:

⊕ Trust others enough to reveal your thinking and/or feelings about something that matters to you

⊕ Discover the diversity in your own story, seek out others' stories

⊕ Share a meal with people you might otherwise avoid

⊕ Become an advocate for others

MIND calls us to explore

The point? To discover new ways of thinking that expand our mindset about God and the systems that hold us.

Practices:

⊕ Think theologically by asking "why does this matter?" and "what is God saying to me through this?"

⊕ Ask yourself "why do I do what I do?" What are the assumptions behind your choices or decisions?

⊕ Experiment with new ways of doing things—read a book or listen to music you would usually avoid

3 The Leadership Landscape:
What is your rhythm

Finding your place on the Leadership Landscape sets you up to grow as a leader that grows a faith community.

Christian leadership is about growing deep, bold, consequential faith.

By the third day on the Inca Trail as I leaned on my poles to take each step, I realized I could tell who in our group was walking in front of me or coming up behind without taking my eyes off the ground. This was a valuable skill as I was going downhill at a steep pace on 3,000 rocky steps. Not only did I have my own rhythm, so did everyone else and I could hear it! In fact you could have lined up our group of 22 people pretty much by age from 12 to 70+ to know how fast we walked. I was reminded how much we need to be in multi-generational groups to understand the fullness of life. In our group, there was as much respect for Peter, the young person who energized us as he eagerly led the way, as there was for the beautiful German couple who arrived at camp after dark each night teaching us about perseverance and inner strength.

Our Peruvian guides and porters, who did not speak English, offered their own gifts to our little community as they sat laughing while we played games in our tents and reflected on the journey each evening. The leadership gift here is to get a new rhythm by getting out of your generational and cultural group. We need to spend time with a wider age group if we really want to be a faithful community. Take this seriously. The church is the one place where five generations have the potential to be in community at the same time.

How are you doing with your rhythm? Is your work-life pace sustainable? Would others who know you well agree with your perspective? Can you breathe at the pace you are going? Have you slowed down a little each month or year until you now find it hard to get through the day? Or do you run from morning to night, or even later, on adrenaline because you love what you do, yet realize the pace is over the top and unsustainable?

All leaders fall somewhere on the grid as we struggle to live a centered life. Notice we do not use the word "balanced" because we have yet to meet a leader who can pull that off as a way of life. In our imaginations we see a balanced life as a day, week, month, or year where everything is as it should be: daily prayer, devotions, and study; daily exercise and healthy eating; daily quality time with our partner and/or children; and of course a clean house, mowed lawn, and full-time job. Whew!

We prefer the word "centered." We love what Oswaldo taught us on the Inca Trail: we each

have to get a rhythm, our own rhythm. We each need a rhythm that makes sense within the context of The Disciple Frame, our call, season of life, and expectations of the place or places in which we serve.

During a time of great change like the one we are living and leading in, the pressure to keep up along with the expectation to be on the cutting edge has many leaders gasping for breath like we were pre-Oswaldo.

In fact as we have listened to leaders, we can group them into four quadrants along two axes. This is what LEAD calls the Leadership Landscape. While most people resent being grouped into what feel like "boxes," we encourage you to be open to understanding what LEAD is doing and why.

First, leaders are grouped to better understand the current landscape of those called and committed to serving in Christian communities. This gives you an awareness of your own leadership as you make a plan to grow.

Second, this offers us a shared language as we move forward together.

Finally, it helps to have clarity around the four Growth Indicators and how they effectively support leaders in all areas of the Leadership Landscape.

Take a moment to look at the image below. Notice the four quadrants formed by the axes running from top to bottom and side to side. Before you turn the page, take a guess about where you might place yourself and your congregation.

THE LEADERSHIP LANDSCAPE DIAGRAM

The range between Deep, Bold, Consequential Faith and Complacent Faith.

This is not a judgment on faithfulness. It is a statement with a bias toward action. Ask, "How is faith being lived out?"

The range between Innovative and Cautious.

This axis describes the willingness of leaders or faith communities to experiment, run pilot projects, try new ideas, or test their call compared with their need to maintain their prior way of life, to play it safe, and to manage people's expectations. Ask, "Is there space to create new ministries that reach beyond our current way of life?"

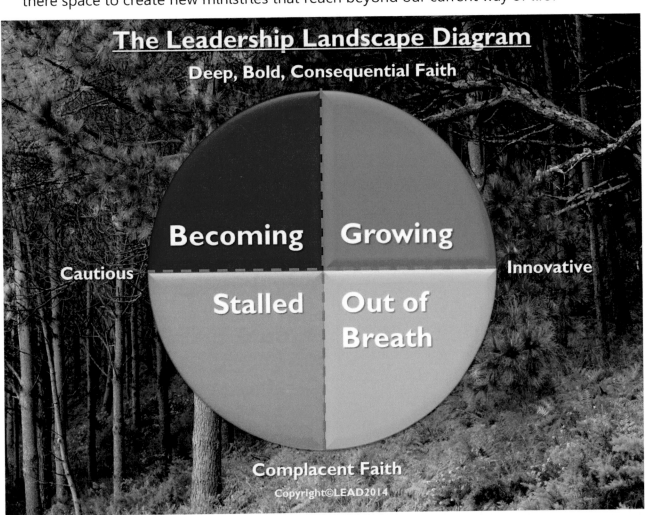

So where did you see yourself on the diagram?

There is a fine line between different leadership behaviors, especially between the Out of Breath and Stalled leaders. In many cases it does not take much to shift a leader into a different quadrant on the landscape.

This is actually good news. Most of the leaders in the church right now are either Stalled or Out of Breath but with a little intentionality they could move into Becoming or Growing. Growth is a choice made by individuals to practice new behaviors, to build new skills, to be open to God in new ways, and to expand their way of thinking. Growth may feel awkward at first, like learning to ride a bike, but everyone can choose to grow, or not to grow, in their faith.

Lifelong learning is critical. Leaders who have been successful with a particular way of leading in the past risk getting stuck there. Without ongoing learning, leaders may think they have it all figured out. But in fact the more we think we know, the harder it is to grow. When we keep doing exactly what we have done in the past, the likelihood of it being successful is slim.

Changes in leadership practices may feel uncomfortable to the community as well. There may actually be push back against new behavior from leaders. In cases like this, it helps when the community can grow with the leader at a pace they can manage.

Leaders cannot grow alone.
Growth that ultimately influences others does not happen in isolation; it is a sign of leadership strength to seek out learning.

Some ways to find community for learning:
⊕ Spiritual guides
⊕ Coaches
⊕ Mentors
⊕ Covenant groups
⊕ Retreats
⊕ Immersion experiences
⊕ Worship

Take a closer look at the four Quadrants in the Leadership Landscape Diagram.

The descriptions of the leadership attributes are generalizations and it is possible you will find yourself and your congregation somewhere between one or more quadrants. Remember, this is to help you identify your own starting place. This is not a destination nor is it prophetic in any way. It is the beginning of the analysis and represents LEAD's best thinking at this time. New iterations will develop based on the insights you share. Having said that, this starting place offers a path forward. LEAD is committed to walking that path with leaders who want to grow. Here is a summary of the quadrants before moving on to the four Growth Indicators.

BECOMING - Leading to live

⊕ May be spiritual but not religious
⊕ May be new to leadership due to change in life stage
⊕ Are passionate about social issues & want to make a difference with their lives

Learn by:
⊕ Volunteering with non-profits, responding to human need and suffering
⊕ Maximizing social media for learning/relationships
⊕ Immersion trips, mission trips, projects

Leadership Style: Networking

GROWING - Living with purpose

⊕ Highly committed to personal growth
⊕ Intentionally grow people of all ages
⊕ Take risks, are innovative, and are discerning vision

Learn by:
⊕ Personal coaching, mentoring or spiritual guide
⊕ Regular continuing education, spiritual practices, and constant reading, prayer, and discernment
⊕ Immersion trips, pilgrimages, responding to suffering and needs in our world

Leadership Style: Casting Vision

STALLED - Done learning

⊕ Think they know everything they need to know and ignore statistics as irrelevant to their setting
⊕ Resist change
⊕ May look more to the past than to the future

Learn by:
⊕ Looking to past models and methods as preferred
⊕ Doing the same kind of continuing education year after year or none at all
⊕ Attending denominational events or out of duty to others

Leadership Style: Authoritative

OUT OF BREATH - Learning to lead

⊕ Are often tired, over-worked, indecisive
⊕ Experience spiritual exhaustion
⊕ Have been "through it" in this or past congregations, or in work and/or family life

Learn by:
⊕ Avoiding conflict, often over-functioning
⊕ Little or no continuing education
⊕ Listening to other leaders, peer groups, struggling to implement what is learned

Leadership Style: Consensus

Copyright©LEAD2014

Four Growth Indicators for Individuals

The four Growth Indicators work for leaders in all four quadrants of the Leadership Landscape regardless of age or season of life. They are behaviors that can intentionally shape our lives. You can do a quick self-assessment by asking yourself the four questions in this box:

⊕ Who have I <u>listened</u> to in the last week inside the faith community and in the neighborhood that keep me tuned in to what God is doing in this place?

⊕ What is my rhythm for prayer and reflection that is helping me wake up to what God is doing for a faith-<u>centered</u> life?

⊕ What ideas or concepts am I <u>exploring</u> that get me excited about learning or digging down into new thinking?

⊕ How am I <u>connected</u> to people who are unlike myself or to a diverse community that is helping me move out of my comfort zone?

Interestingly enough, the best antidote for burnout is most often not more rest or time off but the opportunity to learn and try new things. Taking our own growth seriously is the greatest gift we can give our family, faith life, and work life. A commitment to our own personal growth has a direct impact on the community we serve.

One of the biggest mistakes professional leaders can make is to believe we are saving our congregation money by not taking continuing education. In fact this is how we begin losing traction as leaders and within congregations. The cost of not learning is greater than the money that would have been spent. LEAD recommends including a line item in the budget to invest in growing all leaders.

LEAD's research has shown that there is a gap between what leaders know or learn and what they actually do with it. The leaders we interviewed talked about the helpful information they had learned but never used. Imagine what would happen if we could actually implement new learning? From our research, we have found that the top three things keeping leaders from trying new behaviors are:

1. Lack of personal courage or confidence
2. Fear of making people mad
3. Lack of clarity on exactly what to do

This book and the additional books in the series seek to be helpful to leaders who strive to gain the confidence and courage to ask hard questions, experiment, and innovate. During times of rapid change, it is actually safer to take risks than to continue doing what we have always done. It has been said that fear is the opposite of faith yet we find that they often go hand in hand. While we are faithfully following God's call, we often experience gut-wrenching fear. This is a healthy fear that reminds us we are not in control. However when fear paralyzes us, it may take baby steps and a few wins to move forward. Every win will build confidence for the next effort and the momentum will grow. This is discussed further in the conclusion of this book.

We have more resources than ever before to help us schedule our time but it is up to us to set our priorities. Effective leaders realize that time management is really about energy management and having clear purpose and values. It means getting into a rhythm of rest and work.

Build on your strengths.

The four Growth Indicators are behaviors that take practice. Some behaviors will feel more "like you" than others. Start with those. This asset based approach identifies where leaders feel strongest because as we align our lives in one area, it makes growth in the other areas easier. This is not meant to promote a one-sided leadership style. Instead, as leaders take seriously their own

capacity to love God more deeply by practicing in one part of The Disciple Frame, they will become stronger. This strength allows leaders to challenge themselves to take on areas or practices that might have felt less comfortable at the beginning.

The gifts of the generations and cultures are immeasurable and too often ignored.

As we look at each of the four Growth Indicators it is important to recognize the gifts every leader receives when stepping out of a familiar worldview. We have blinders and filters that come from our own experience and regardless of how open we may hope to become, we can never fully set our own perspectives aside. We need people from different cultures (geographic, socioeconomic, ethnic, etc.) and different generations to teach us how they understand scripture and the world. These are the jewels that help leaders see the world a little more like God sees it.

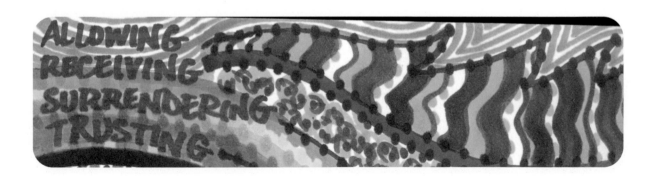

The four Growth Indicators for Leaders and Faith Communities

The Disciple Frame and the four Growth Indicators work for individuals and for communities. Congregations, just like people, have behaviors that grow the mission and behaviors that limit or even stop growth. In order of likelihood, the three most common triggers for change in a congregation are:

1. A change in pastoral leadership or leaders taking a new call
2. A crisis (becoming too small to pay a pastor is the most common one)
3. A critical mass of people, including the lead pastor and other staff, who are willing to do the hard work of making change

However, the most effective way of making change is #3! When leaders move into mission out of a sense of God's call, adapting to their context with experiments and integrity, change can be organic. A clear understanding of "why" something new is happening can help with the transition.

Change happens at the speed of trust, however a new pastor does not have to wait for years before making changes in a faith community. Every new leader has a short window of opportunity to make changes early in their tenure—yet it is never too late to ask new questions, following God into the future. The four Growth Indicators are behaviors that can strategically unfold one step at a time.

A Call and Response

The four Growth Indicators are meaningless unless they elicit both a call to grow and the act of growth. In other words, just learning something is not enough. Putting the growth indicators into practice includes concrete, visible behavior change. The overall theme of the Growth Indicators is outwardly focused.

> If you want to change how a person thinks, give up. You cannot change how another thinks. Give them a tool the use of which will gradually cause them over time to think differently. – Buckminster Fuller

Use the chart on the next page to catch a glimpse of how this could play out in your own life or in the life of your congregation. Remember, behavior change begins with the staff, elected leaders, and all team leaders.

Nothing happens without leadership.

FOUR GROWTH INDICATORS
CALL & RESPONSE CHART

Call and Response	Individual Growth Indicators	Community Growth Indicators
Response to Listening	⊕ Works with a professional coach or has a mentor ⊕ Mentors others ⊕ Asks questions, listens for response ⊕ Empathizes with different perspectives	⊕ Trains, equips others to listen ⊕ Builds relationships by listening to people in the neighborhood before offering help ⊕ Expects new people to come with needs and gifts unlike their own ⊕ Advocates for all voices to be heard
Response to Centering	⊕ Works with a spiritual guide ⊕ Engages in regular faith practices like worship, prayer, study, service, etc. ⊕ Shares faith and faith story with others ⊕ Talks about God in daily life	⊕ Trains and equips others to lead meaningful worship, music, and preaching ⊕ Lives out Core Beliefs, Core Convictions, and Core Practices; shares them on the website, Facebook, etc. ⊕ Knows the answer to: Why do we exist as a church?
Response to Exploring	⊕ Belongs to peer networks that challenge assumptions ⊕ Reads, listens to audio books and podcasts, or watches videos constantly ⊕ Questions the status quo ⊕ Pursues answers to questions, researches as a life-long learner	⊕ Understands their God narrative with a theology that reflects a loving God ⊕ Understands clearly the role for staff and council ⊕ Encourages generosity through Core Practices ⊕ Makes it possible for new things to happen within Core Values and congregational Purpose
Response to Connecting	⊕ Goes on international or local pilgrimages or immersions ⊕ Learns new languages or embraces new cultures ⊕ Listens and embraces perspectives beyond their own or those they may disagree with ⊕ Respects and defends differences	⊕ Has zero tolerance for racism, genderism, or any other "ism" ⊕ Creates Core Practices for sharing power, stories, and understanding of God's story ⊕ Makes intentional effort to expand people's worldview

Maximizing the Call and Response with Coaches, Spiritual Guides, Mentors, and Peer Networks

While LEAD provides a wide variety of resources and seminars, the four most helpful tools we have to offer are:

1. Professional Coaches
2. Spiritual Guides
3. Mentors
4. Peer Networks

Coaching:
Professional coaching increases self understanding, provides personal accountability, and makes space for new insights. The more deeply you connect to your God-given gifts, the more effectively you can grow into God's vision for you. Coaching supports leaders as they identify strengths and challenges, relate them to ideal competencies for leadership and pastoral care, and develop strategies for growth.

All leadership requires the ability to cast vision, communicate it clearly, and build support for it. The stresses of transformational change raise the stakes and make it difficult to create healthy teams and overcome resistance to change. It's essential that leaders develop high-level skills in these areas. Coaching can make all the difference as leaders take up these new skills, overcome existing congregational paradigms that are slowing down mission, and create an outwardly focused ministry. It is very hard to do this work without the accompaniment of a coach who offers personal accountability.

The inertia of congregational life can easily trump the good intentions of a leader.

Professional coaches are people with training, often a master's degree, and experience with asking questions. The coach works to strengthen their client typically without sharing their own preferences or opinions. Generally people pay for a coach's time, meeting for six months to three years.

Spiritual Guide:
It is likely that we can all name parents, grandparents, or other caring people as instrumental in our faith formation. Having a professional spiritual guide comes closer to a coaching relationship. The primary difference is that the spiritual guide has been trained to raise awareness of God moving in your life. Through reflection, prayer, and questions, a spiritual guide brings the gifts of ancient mystics, historic theologians, and faith practices into your life.

While some spiritual guides work at no cost or for a donation to their community, most include a regular fee. People often meet with a spiritual guide during a particular season of their lives (like the first year of a new pastoral call). Others will meet regularly or sporadically over many years as they continue to develop their awareness of God moving in their life with a deepening maturity of faith.

Mentoring:
We have all benefited from thinking partners who may or may not realize the impact they are having on our

own worldview. Mentoring takes this to a more strategic level with an intentional investment in building capacity in another person. The best mentors are likely the ones we seek out ourselves.

However, there are times when a mentor is "recommended" to us for our personal development or "provided" for us as part of a career change. The true benefit of mentoring is the investment someone is making in another person's growth. The commitment of time, along with encouragement, wisdom, and resources, is usually part of the process. Mentors readily share their own experiences and offer advice making this time valuable for leadership formation.

In the best mentoring relationships, everyone grows. For this reason, there is usually no financial cost for mentoring.

Peer Networks: Groups of people with similar passions, vocation, or call that meet regularly are life-giving. These are people we feel "get us" and provide us with a safe place where we can feel fully known and loved. Everyone needs these kinds of communities where they can process their experiences, be held accountable by peers, and learn from others.

Peer Networks are a lot like mentoring with the added benefit of a group component. Networks meet face-to-face or with digital tools. They may be closed to new people or ever expanding to include new people into the group. There may be a small fee, a

facilitator, or some structure for making decisions, but they are seldom hierarchical.

The healthiest leaders experience all four of these support systems at varying times in their life. They seek out the kind of support they need recognizing that it is their personal responsibility to grow.

So where should you start?

The chapters that follow illustrate the ways the four Growth Indicators are expressed in Growing, Out of Breath, Stalled, or Becoming congregations. The Growth Indicators are used as leverage points, as tools for gradually growing people and communities deeper in faith. It is common for individuals and congregations to find themselves in different quadrants for each Growth Indicator, perhaps even Stalled in one and Growing in another.

The LEAD Congregational Assessment is a good place to start. This online assessment tool for congregations is available at waytolead.org/assessment and described in detail on pages 75-77 of this book. The LEAD Assessment does not measure everything; it focuses on the four Growth Indicators described in this book offering crucial metrics for establishing baselines on each.

4 Four Growth Indicators and Growing Congregations:
Living with purpose

When we are on a spiritual pilgrimage, some behaviors matter more than others.

By the afternoon of the third day, I was in the groove of hiking enough to notice the others on the trail. We were hiking in the prime season, the warmest part of the Peruvian winter. There were people from all over the world walking past me speaking many different languages. Picture an endless trail of tiny little steps. This is what we were going down pretty much all day. Now picture me stepping to the side every few minutes while a group of German or Japanese or English or Australian hikers went barreling past. Occasionally, as they would stop to rest, I would actually pass them sitting on the side of the trail laughing or gasping for air. It was sort of like being on the highway because over the course of the day we would take turns passing each other as we settled into our own hiking patterns.

> The sacred valley calls for leaders who are on a pilgrimage living with purpose as they listen to God.

After hours of hiking, I began to feel like I had a relationship with these people, with some of them anyway. I was struck by the attitudes of other hikers. There were some who acted like they owned the trail with no acknowledgement of the sacred path much less the rest of us. There were others who were helping total strangers get up when they fell, which was easy to do on the steps. Over the course of the day some people who started out as strangers ended up as friends.

Even now after all the time that has gone by since I hiked the trail, I still wonder about the diverse ways people experienced this pilgrimage. There is a "way of being" in the world that says a lot about who we are. There is a respect for the sacred. There is hospitality to strangers. There is a joy that comes from being together on the journey.

In this liminal space, some people were missing the moment. The liminal principle of the Gospel reminds us that God works through disorienting human experiences, not just on the Inca Trail but in the reflexive process of shared experiences. The language we use, our openness to new insights, our way of being together all ultimately open us up to experience the movement of God. This is the holy of holies, human beings awake to God moving in our own hearts. There are special places in our lives where this kind of God-awareness is even more real. Too often we miss it because we are focused on ourselves, even in the Sacred Valley.

Growing congregations are finding ways to wake up to God's presence.

The behaviors of Growing congregations serve as snapshots of what happens when we are open to God's presence and as invitations to catch up with the Holy Spirit in this changing world.

Be warned: We miss the point when we think that what is contagious about growing congregations is their worship style. It is more likely that the draw is their authentic worship of a living God. Trying to duplicate another congregation's way of being may not work in your context. Attractional ministry is not the goal. Focus instead on discipleship, on authentic relationships, and on making meaning out of life.

GROWING LEADERS CAST VISION

Leadership in today's changing world means experimenting. Leaders with a willingness to try new things through courageous pilot projects or a few small bets will learn more than others as they sense God's call. Everything becomes a "so where is God in this and what did we learn here?" conversation. Growing leaders build on these learnings to develop a wealth of resources that inform each other. Tinkering, playing with ideas, and permission to fail are what it takes to spark an epiphany.

For example, consider a leader that experiments with something out of the box like helping parents make their own household plan to grow faith in their family. The leader helps families set family goals and provides resources that allow them to do faith formation in the home with the parent taking on the youth minister's role. Through this process, they may unexpectedly discover new models of family faith formation! Even if only five families participate in the pilot project, new things can be learned. The next iteration of the project might be to launch a "School's Out" plan for summer faith formation using what worked best in the earlier pilot. Without the first experiment, they might never have come up with the idea to enrich summer faith formation in a new way. This is *living with purpose*.

> Being heard is so close to being loved that for the average person they are almost indistinguishable.
> *- David Augsburger*

Growing leaders and communities are strong in at least three of the four Growth Indicators:

Listen – Opening the Heart

Growing leaders understand that asking questions is more important than delivering their own opinions. They seek out people who do not speak up in large groups knowing that they too have much to offer. Growing leaders have a regular discipline of one-on-one relational meetings with a wide variety of people, not just those who give the most money, have the loudest voices, or complain a lot. They get their best information for making adaptive change by connecting the dots between what they have heard from God, from people in the congregation, and from people in the neighborhood. A commitment to listening helps leaders focus on what matters most. This is a skill to be learned as we set aside our own biases and filters to pay full attention to what we hear.

Leaders in these congregations are intentionally listening in real time, as close to the ground as possible. This includes all three types of listening—to God, to the congregation, and to the neighborhood. This happens through the Tune In process, on-going relationships in the community, and other strategic networking; it is not a one-time event.

Growing congregations also listen carefully as they evaluate all they do. This means that learning is not based on their best memory from the past but on what just happened, with whom, and why. The more involved the whole community can be in evaluation, the more likely listening will become a way of life leading to gifts for the future.

Listening outside the congregation, in the neighborhood, and in the world is crucial. Leaders of Growing congregations say that listening beyond regular attenders is critically important too. It strengthens preaching and teaching in ways that are relevant and answer the real questions people are asking.

> It is not enough to be busy; so are the ants. The question is: what are we busy about?
> - Henry David Thoreau

Social media has opened up a whole new way of listening. Through Facebook and Twitter posts, blog articles, and YouTube videos, the world just got louder and more available. Leaders of Growing congregations take this seriously and strategically participate in all forms of communication.

Even a short conversation with someone in person or through social media can change a life. Think about Philip and the Eunuch (Acts 8) or Peter and Cornelius (Acts 10) when a few hours or days changed the course of history.

Center – Renewing the Soul

Growing leaders are intentional about their own spiritual practices. They are committed to making space in their busy lives for regular prayer, study, and growth as followers of Jesus Christ. In fact, they strive to model time apart with their closest leaders or alone to discern where God is calling them just as Jesus did. The practice of Dwelling in the Word, of leading out of silence, and a real sense of walking with God are tangible when you meet with these leaders.

Growing Christian communities have a clear purpose. That is to say, they know why their congregations exist. They have an answer to the question, "if our congregation disappeared tomorrow, what would the neighborhood miss?"

There is an understanding of their three sets of core values: Core Beliefs, Core Convictions, and Core Practices. See the LEAD resource, *Wake Up Guide*, for more information (waytolead.org/wake-up-process).

Decision-making about experiments is always aligned with the purpose of the congregation. The core values create a playing field for exploring new models without stepping out of bounds. This centeredness allows for new things to happen in line with the congregation's identity similar to the way The Disciple Frame shapes our own faith life.

Explore – Shifting the Mind

Growing leaders see learning as an adventure. They are clear that they do not have all the answers and are open to learning from unexpected sources. Because of their commitment to learning, these leaders are able to unlock new ways of thinking and make linkages that have not been made in the past. Whether intentionally or not, as they try these new experiments they are practicing the Blue Ocean Strategy.

The Blue Ocean Strategy encourages us to resist the urge to compete with other similar "markets" like rivals fighting over a shrinking pool of resources. Instead, we each seek to discover new space that is ripe for growth. This opens the way for innovation and creativity, making competition irrelevant as new connections are formed and new frameworks or tools discovered.

Innovative leadership is excellent at making adaptive changes and is at the frontier of emerging theologies, practices, and communities.

The difference between an adaptive change and a technical change is important. Technical changes are those we already know how to make whereas adaptive changes require new ways of thinking, experimenting, and connecting the dots. *The Practice of Adaptive Leadership*, a book by Ronald Heifetz, Alexander Grashow and Marty Linsky, clearly outlines this for the

> We are what we repeatedly do. Excellence, then, is not an act but a habit.
> *- Aristotle*

marketplace, but these same practices are needed in our faith communities.

Expanding our welcome to new people offers a great example of the difference between technical and adaptive change. "Hospitality lite" involves technical changes. We do what we know how to do (coffee and cookies after worship, for example) but after looking at it through the eyes of a visitor, we may add a sugar free or gluten free option. "Hospitality deep" involves adaptive changes (ones that we may not know how to make) by considering the needs of people who are not yet in the church like Latino families or Millennials. In order to make these adaptive changes, we would need to listen to people in the group we hope to connect with, explore possible changes, experiment with new practices, etc. Inevitably, some things that we thought would work, will fail. Adaptive change always makes room for failure as part of growth. More information about adaptive change can be found on the LEAD blog at waytolead.org/blog.

Growing leaders are always highly committed to personal development. They seek out mentors, coaches, and guides who can "make them smarter." They recognize what they need to learn and go after it. These leaders have an honest self-awareness that makes them lifelong learners. In addition, people who are always learning surround themselves with others who are learning. They understand that being a

Christian leader means not just living as a disciple but discipling others.

Pastors who are constantly reading, wrestling with questions, and encouraging experiments within the congregation's core values are better preachers and teachers. Their personal growth shows in their ability to inspire others. They are usually team builders inviting others into their thinking and generating ongoing dialog about topics that push others deeper in their own faith. This is true for Growing congregations as well.

Growing congregations that are willing to explore are asking hard questions about long-held ways of life. Examples include:

⊕ **Re-thinking the culture of governance to allow space for creativity.** Clarity of roles between the pastor(s), staff, council, ministry teams, members, and visitors allows for better decision-making and makes innovation possible. If a new idea has to be approved at multiple levels, creativity is next to impossible.

⊕ **Re-thinking "meetings" in order to free people to do ministry, not just talk about it.** Growing congregations use emerging technology to get the job done faster so people spend less time away from their families doing the "church work" that has often caused their children to resent church. Meetings are happening on Zoom or via Google Hangout, to name a

few free resources. Shared work is kept in Dropbox or other such apps and teams are connected for prayer and sharing through Facebook groups. Often this results in deeper relationships as it frees people to live out their passion to do ministry.

These are only a few of the ways Growing leaders are exploring our world.

Connect – Building Strength

Growing leaders know people come to church for many reasons but what keeps them there are relationships and a sense of belonging. When people feel loved and have an opportunity to love each other, they are meeting and being like Jesus.

> **CONNECT**
> He loves righteousness and justice; the earth is full of the steadfast love of the Lord.
> - Psalm 33:5

In the book *Generations Together*, the authors share important research that says people feel they belong to a community when they participate in intergenerational experiences. They remind us how "Abraham Maslow famously demonstrated that belonging is a basic human need." Humans cannot thrive unless they feel they are connected to a community. In some cases, this is even more basic than the need for safety or self-preservation, as with those who stay in abusive relationships. People place a very high value on a sense of community. This has great potential for the church today. In a fascinating study by James Kouzes and Barry Posner which is summarized in their book, *The Truth about Leadership*, a commitment to a community is shown to be driven more by the personal values of the members than by the corporate values of the community. Kouzes and Posner discovered that:

> people commit to organizations when those organizations understand and honor what the people value most. When people value a sense of belonging, organizations need to be building spaces that are hospitable and create a warm sense of community.

Growing congregations are highly committed to attending to relationships. In the past, the pattern for faith formation was Believe/Behave/Belong. First we encouraged belief in Jesus Christ. Then we would talk about aligning our behavior to follow Christ's commandments. Finally we would commit to belonging by becoming a church member. Today people are following a different path: Belong/Believe/Behave. This is actually more similar to the way Jesus called people together. Jesus reached out to those that were marginalized by society. He showed them God's love and that they belonged to God. Out of authentic connections, people believed. They didn't need to believe in order to have God's love. Jesus first let these individuals know that they belonged and that He loved them regardless of their behavior. It was only after this that people chose to change the way in which they behaved. Today it is out of belonging and then belief that we decide to change how we behave.

Working out of their comfort zone

Growing congregations are not afraid to take a stand on behalf of human rights and suffering. They are willing to enter into touchy subjects that call for Christian advocacy and justice even at the risk of upsetting a few people, if the issues at hand align with their purpose and values.

These congregations are ready to make incremental changes for the sake of God's mission understanding that it is often more successful to run pilot projects and try experiments than to make giant shifts in the system—unless of course, they have a critical mass of people who are committed to making these leaps of faith. We have seen growing congregations take risks in forming strategic partnerships to further their mission. We have seen others embrace ethnic, cultural, or socio-economic diversity as they have lived into values of deep hospitality.

In the end, the word "growing" is not always about the number of people in worship or the amount of money given; it is more about discipleship, integrity, and purpose.

The Leadership Style that defines Growing is "Casting Vision."

Purpose is a concrete, concise picture of what God is calling the congregation to do. The bigger the vision, the more important it is that the purpose be clear enough for others to repeat. The goal is for the purpose to be widely owned and to compel people toward new goals. Discerning purpose requires deep listening to God. This listening moves beyond the congregation's current way of life and capacity. It includes faithful mission in the community and world to draw people of faith into a wider view of God. A purposeful vision is always about being more than what we already are. A purpose statement can be vetted among key leaders to hone the language for clarity and to test what we think we are hearing in order to build confidence that it is God who is speaking.

Communicating purpose takes a consistent voice for it to have traction in the community. Bill Hybels, who serves as Senior Pastor at Willow Creek, has said that vision leaks and needs to be re-cast every 21 days. This applies to purpose as well. In his book *Ax.i.om* he argues:

> Some leaders believe that if they fill people's vision buckets all the way to the top one time, those buckets will stay full forever. But the truth is, people's buckets have holes of varying sizes in their bottoms. As a result, vision leaks out. You or I could deliver a mind-blowing, God-honoring talk on Sunday that leaves everyone revved up to go change the world, but by Tuesday, many people have forgotten they were even in church the previous weekend. Unbelievable, huh?

This is exactly the same for purpose. People need to be reminded why the church exists, even as often as monthly. The more outward the purpose is, the more crucial the repetition is to overcome our default tendency to care for the people we are already in relationship with. In addition, we know from the research cited in *The Vanishing Neighbor* by Mark Dunkelman that people can only manage 150 relationships at a time based on our brain capacity. This means congregations can easily top-out unless there are mechanisms built into the system to share in the caring. Systems like small group ministries allow for a congregation to grow with an outward purpose and remain intimate at the same time.

A clear God-given purpose will provide hope, moving an Out of Breath or even Stalled congregation forward in mission. Yet it must be continuously re-cast or re-taught until people are repeating the purpose in their own words. Leaders of Growing congregations are learning to clarify, teach, and communicate purpose as a way of life.

5 Four Growth Indicators and Out of Breath Congregations:
Learning to lead

When we are on a spiritual pilgrimage, the community really matters.

> The sacred valley can wear leaders out as they hit roadblocks of conflict, decline, uncertainty, or a lack of confidence on the pilgrimage.

The rhythm of movement and rest was evident in all the hikers as a way of surviving the trail. It became clear that those who were willing to take advice from the guides and engaging with people they would never have known if they were not hiking the same trail were having more fun. They were faster to catch their breath because they were supporting each other. Somehow the very feeling of being "in it together" made the hard parts doable.

Some got sick, maybe from water that was not boiled long enough or maybe from the stress and exhaustion of the hiking. Some were so tired that eating the evening meal was too much effort so they lost weight on the trip while others loved the five course dinners and gained weight! We all responded to the conditions of the hike in different ways.

As hard as it was, we could feel God drawing us together. None of us had done this before and we had a lot to learn. It would have been a whole different journey if we had not taken care of each other, laughed and cried together, and shared our supplies. The gift of the community outweighed anything any one of us could have done alone.

The tents provided an even more intimate experience as we shared this small space with one other person. It was this person who knew how we were doing without asking as each tent became like a little "family."

While most of the experience was shared as a community, we did not do the whole hike side by side. We each had our own pace and our own rhythm. It was a gift to be able to stop and breathe or take pictures when it felt right to me. I was not locked into specific "Kodak-moment" lookouts or a designated "break time" on an agenda. The privilege of setting my own pace within the supportive community really helped.

I discovered a centeredness in the tension between being together and being alone that allowed me to experience God walking with me in the Sacred Valley.

Within minutes they were bickering over who of them would end up the greatest. But Jesus intervened: "Kings like to throw their weight around and people in authority like to give themselves fancy titles. It's not going to be that way with you. Let the senior among you become like the junior; let the leader act the part of the servant."

- Luke 22:24-26 (MSG)

OUT OF BREATH LEADERS BUILD CONSENSUS

Most of the leaders in the church today are out of breath. Leadership in a changing world is exhausting. It involves motivating, organizing, honing, and coordinating the efforts of a wide variety of people around a shared purpose and values. But what are the purpose and values?

We are all part of a worldwide, history-wide God-story that is bigger than we can grasp. The world is changing and many congregations are shrinking every year. Life is hard to predict and there are many obstacles to any goal we might set. Sometimes it is hard to know what the "right" goals are for this place and time. It can feel like some people have all the answers and others don't.

Sometimes we take the advice we are given or trust our guts when we are making important decisions. Yet authors Chip Heath and Dan Heath in their book *Decisive* share research that proves that our guts are full of questionable advice and so are many of our friends! If we can't trust our guts, then who or what can we trust?

If any of this resonates with you, you are in good company. Most of the leaders in the church today are Out of Breath. The fast pace of change in our world has shifted the landscape and we cannot keep up. The church of our childhood or, in the case of the pastor, the church we were trained to serve is not bearing as much fruit as it once was.

> Listen, are you breathing just a little, and calling it a life?
> - *Mary Oliver*

There is deep concern among faithful leaders in this quadrant for making change without sacrificing members and for preserving what matters most. They are willing to try new things, but what? It often feels like every new thing gets a disapproval rating from the major stakeholders. Leaders are worn out and they over function just to try to stabilize the congregation. They feel like they are too busy to invest in their own faith life, leaving them spiritually empty. And nobody needs more conflict or negative attitudes.

The whole environment is eroding their confidence. To grow, Out of Breath leaders need a safe space to experiment but the current culture does not welcome their creativity. These leaders are often people who are *learning to lead* for the first time. The world they were trained for does not exist. Keeping up with the rapid development of new technologies and ways of thinking makes them feel like they are out of step. Even if they disagree with these new trends, they are being challenged to engage in them.

What does hope look like for Out of Breath leaders? Think of the four Growth Indicators as a place to start.

Listen – Opening the Heart

Getting out of their comfort zone for a bigger view of God through a cross-cultural immersion might seem like an odd recommendation but it works! Out of Breath leaders need to step away from their responsibilities long enough to see God moving in a different place in the world. This sparks new imagination for God moving in their own space. Widening their own experiences can be the beginning of visionary leadership.

There is so much to be learned from people of different generations and cultures. Seriously listening to people we would not usually engage with is eye-opening when we suspend judgment and put our own listening filters aside to really understand their point of view. By doing this we can also catch a glimpse of God that we may have missed before. Over time, deep listening can change our own perspective and prayer life.

Center – Renewing the Soul

Spiritual growth happens in many ways. Small covenant groups of faithful people in the same season of life meeting weekly to pray, study, share, and care for each other is a healthy place to begin. Deepening our relationships with each other and God reminds us that it is really God who grows faith.

Intentional work with a spiritual guide or taking up new spiritual practices is essential for leaders who want to grow. In many ways being out of breath is a crisis of faith even if we do not want to admit it. We need to reschedule our lives to include space to notice what the Holy Spirit is doing. Out of a life of deepening prayer and attentiveness we can gain confidence in our own call to lead others.

Explore – Shifting the Mind

How we think about things can keep us stuck. Identifying our own assumptions, questioning unwritten rules, finding a pace that is life-giving, and stretching our thinking with reading, coaching, or new training can provide a wider perspective. Strengthening leadership skills starts with how we think.

We are all more stuck than we realize when it comes to our mindset. We have blind spots, patterns of behaviors, and default responses to life that have been critical to our survival in the past. Some of these ways of being will actually be obstacles to overcome as we lead in a changing world. Most of us cannot make these changes alone. We need the accountability and encouragement that comes from sharing our hearts and prayers with others.

As mentioned on pages 30-31, leaders who draw on the resources of coaches, mentors, spiritual guides, and peer networks have a better chance of regaining momentum. God has designed us for relationship, yet when things get hard we often move inward, leaving behind the very resources that would keep us healthy. Leaders who are committed to moving beyond an Out of Breath posture will want to put personal effort into working with one or more of these individuals as they map their own growth.

Connect – Building Strength

There are two primary connections that will be game changers for leaders who are Out of Breath:

⊕ Deepening discipleship (including physical, spiritual, and mental health)
⊕ Deepening relationships (increasing diversity, integrity, and transparency)

These two paths in a leader's life impact leadership capacity more than anyone realizes. Taking steps toward a deepening faith with intentional spiritual practices including a more physically active lifestyle, good food choices, and portion control actually change our ability to lead. Likewise opening up our circle of relationships to include a wider pool of people, even when it makes us feel vulnerable, results in new inspiration, imagination, and purpose.

Think about Jesus's ministry. What did he actually do? Jesus prayed, asked strategic questions, told meaningful stories, ate and drank with people, invested deeply in a small group, and healed people. Jesus tended the full spectrum of human need—physical, emotional, mental, and spiritual. This is a good place to start in our own ministry and, even more, in our own lives. We have to lead ourselves before we can lead others.

Be honest. How many times have we made resolutions that have not lasted? How many workout programs, healthy diet plans, or other habits have we tried to adopt only to find ourselves right back where we started, or worse? Most of us are notorious for being

> Jesus prayed, asked strategic questions, told meaningful stories, ate and drank with people, invested deeply in a small group, and healed people.

people with good intentions who get derailed by the needs of others or even our own exhaustion. Yet if we want to lead Jesus-style, focusing on our own discipleship is step one.

Clarifying our own passions, God-given call, and values is important. In the chapter on *Finding Your Voice* in the book *Leadership Challenge*, Kouzes and Posner pose a series of questions for reflection to help us identify what we care most about. Take some time as you ask yourself these thoughtful questions:

⊕ What do you stand for? Why?
⊕ What do you believe in? Why?
⊕ What are you discontented about? Why?
⊕ What brings you suffering? Why?
⊕ What makes you weep and wail? Why?
⊕ What makes you jump for joy? Why?
⊕ What are you passionate about? Why?
⊕ What keeps you awake at night? Why?
⊕ What has grabbed hold and will not let go? Why?
⊕ What do you want for your life? Why?
⊕ Just what is it that you really care about? Why?

Drawing on Ancient Spiritual Practices

In the Christian community, this kind of reflection is known as *Ignatian Examen*. This and other ancient faith practices encourage us to wake up, to notice what God is doing in our lives through our own life experiences.

When leaders who are Out of Breath start this practice they may begin to notice places where God is moving that they have previously missed due to exhaustion or insecurity. It will give leaders courage to take risks as they remember what it means to be God's people.

It may feel counter intuitive to add things to our already over-burdened lives. This is an invitation to stop doing some of the things that have consumed our time. Escape mechanisms like watching TV, surfing the web, or over-doing it on Facebook, for example, masquerade as relaxation while really just distracting us from exercising self-discipline. Nothing is more life-giving than beginning to notice where God is moving in your life. It may be impossible to truly lead others until we gain a glimpse of God in our own lives.

> A fearful Christian is the person who has not understood the message of Jesus.
> — *Pope Francis*

In the book *Nurture Shock,* the authors acknowledge how hard it is for us to budge from our old habits and proclivities. While it is possible to inspire a few people to change, it's nearly impossible to change a majority of us in any direction. Until we ourselves as leaders have courage to act, we will remain stuck on whatever is easiest to accomplish. These steps can help you inspire change in yourself and in others:

⊕ Listen to your own passions and write out your own goals. Sustaining interest in your own goals is a building block to success. (Listen)

⊕ Avoid distractions by being so committed to the new behaviors that they consume you. (Center)

⊕ Learn new ways to think so you can manage the way you talk to yourself. (Explore)

⊕ Seek support in a community with others ahead of you, heading the same direction you feel called to go. (Connect)

The most compelling thing about the research in the book *Nurture Shock* is that they were testing with kindergartners!

Nurture Shock makes the point that a motivated brain literally operates better and learns more.

This concept of self-motivation fits with the research done by Daniel Pink mentioned in Chapter 1. We share this to encourage you. Striving to make personal behavior changes and leading others is not easy. It takes courage, commitment, and support to change.

Growth is indeed a choice, not an easy one but it is possible. It is a choice that no one can make for another. It comes when connecting to what God is doing in and around us exerts a more powerful tug on us than our old ways of living do. Seldom can we do this alone.

> This is what God the LORD says—
> the Creator of the heavens, who
> stretches them out, who spreads
> out the earth with all that springs
> from it, who gives breath to its
> people, and life to those who walk
> on it: "I, the LORD, have called you
> in righteousness; I will take hold of
> your hand. I will keep you and will
> make you to be a covenant for the
> people and a light for the Gentiles,
> to open eyes that are blind, to
> free captives from prison and to
> release from the dungeon those
> who sit in darkness.
> - *Isaiah 42:5-7 (NIV)*

What would the neighborhood miss if your congregation disappeared tomorrow?

This is a tough question for many faith communities. Throughout the history of our church, we have been so busy taking care of members that we have often missed what God is doing in our own neighborhood. This inward focus results in a shift from where the congregation was when it was originally planted. Most new mission congregations are launched with neighborhood engagement. As the neighborhood evolved, and even more so if members moved farther away, the church ceased to reflect the demographics of the people around it. While this is often an unconscious progression, there are also times when an intentional choice is made to ignore the neighbors who may speak a different language or have a different cultural heritage.

Out of Breath congregations struggle with one or more of the following:

⊕ A disconnect from the neighborhood and/or a disconnect from joining God in responding to human need and suffering. Just providing meeting space for outside groups does not count. (Listen)

⊕ A clear purpose and shared values that align ministry. (Center)

⊕ Paths for people to grow deeper in their faith, small groups for authentic relationships, space to question assumptions, and clear governance that invites experimentation. (Explore)

⊕ Multiple ways for people to be vulnerable with each other for authentic relationships; sustainable intergenerational and cross-cultural relationships with a true focus on hospitality and welcoming all. (Connect)

The four Growth Indicators are an invitation for Out of Breath faith communities to ask new questions about themselves. The Congregational Assessment at waytolead.org/assessment is a valuable tool to help leaders engage others in these conversations. The first step to becoming a

Growing congregation is to know where the congregation is currently located in the sacred valley. Then listening in the neighborhood helps to re-ground the congregation in the very place God has planted them for mission. Once these two things are happening, leaders can begin to discern the congregation's purpose and core values. There are three sets of core values operating at the same time and by discerning all three, a congregation can move toward alignment for a more sustainable way of life. Leaders working through this process will benefit from accompaniment by a consultant (who will bring new skills and train leaders) or coach (who helps leaders set and achieve goals).

Scripting the moves to lead change is one of the recommendations from the book *Switch* by Heath and Heath that encourages us to change vague concepts or wishful thinking into concrete goals and actions. There is more on leading change at waytolead.org/blog and in the conclusion of this book.

Governance Changes

Timing is everything for leaders who are guiding congregational change. This includes key decisions like determining what changes to make, in what order, and how fast. For example, leaders who start the change process by taking on governance issues will usually add more anxiety into the system. Of course re-thinking governance is a key to sustaining change, but it is seldom the most effective place to begin moving a congregation from Out of Breath to Growing.

Having effectively listened into the neighborhood and clarified purpose and all three types of values, a congregation is ready to address governance. Different types of governance are helpful for different size congregations.

The size of the worshiping community will dictate the ways ministry happens best and how behaviors need to shift to accommodate a new, or not so new, size. Leaders who are living with models for decision-making (governance), staffing (including volunteer staff), and expectations (programs, power dynamics, etc.) that were effective at one stage of life but not aligned with current congregational size face important decisions.

There are many resources available for congregations when they are ready to begin working on governance. In the meantime, there are three key changes that can be made quickly to relieve pressure at council meetings. These three changes can become the work of the church council while a new team of people focus on the Tune In Process (waytolead.org/tune-in).

First, if you are not already doing so, move to the use of a consent agenda. A consent agenda allows routine items not requiring discussion to be considered for approval together as one agenda item. This can save precious time in a meeting. Typical items on the consent agenda include:

⊕ Approval of the minutes

⊕ Final approval of proposals or reports that the council has already discussed

⊕ Routine matters such as appointments to committees

⊕ Staff work requiring approval

⊕ Committee reports provided for information only without an action item

The key to introducing a consent agenda to a council that has come to expect lengthy discussions on these items is to assure them that any item on the consent agenda can easily be moved to the discussion agenda. Anyone can make this request and it does not require a vote. The other key is to utilize newly freed up time to do one or more of these things:

⊕ Share faith practices

⊕ Tend the congregation's purpose

⊕ Set new goals

⊕ Review metrics of past goals

⊕ Discuss material for council growth like a book, article, or video

The point here is to reduce meetings to no more than two hours with one hour dedicated to managing the business of the church and the other to growing the leadership of the church.

The second key change, without a full overhaul of the congregation's governance, is to clarify roles. Understanding the work of the staff (paid and volunteer), the work of the council, and the work shared between the two is crucial. Dan Hotchkiss does a great job of describing these roles in detail in his book, *The Art of Governance.*

Finally, and most importantly, is agreement on the answer to the question "Who owns the church?" The church is different from other organizations we belong to, give money to, or invest our time in because it is gathered to carry out God's mission, not our own. The short answer to this question is always, God owns the church. The conversations that follow will take time and trust-building as people come to terms with their role as servant rather than owner. The sooner these three governance factors are established and agreed upon, the faster the congregation can move into mission.

On a related note, moving from Out of Breath to Growing requires letting go of certain styles of leadership as they relate to programs. Programs from the past may be slowing things down or even getting in the way of new opportunities. The church of the future will have fewer programs and more meaningful relationships. Reducing the time spent talking about ministry and increasing the time spent experiencing God in daily life is part of this shift. Committee work brought meaning to people in the past in ways that are no longer true today.

Congregational Size Influences Leadership Behavior

It is helpful for Out of Breath leaders and congregations to take an honest look at their current size. Susan Beaumont, a congregational coach and consultant, groups congregations by attendance and budget. If your congregation has grown or declined by even 20%, you may be using a leadership model with behaviors that no longer fit.

This chart is adapted from Beaumont's work. Where do you see your congregation?

	Attendance	Budget
Family	0-100	$100K-150K
Pastoral	100-250	$150K-400K
Multi-Cell	250-400	$400K-1M
Professional	400-800	$1M-2M
Strategic	800-1200	$2M-4M
Matrix	1200-1800	$4M+

We ask this question not to get distracted by metrics (more on that beginning on page 85) but to trigger a mindset conversation essential for Out of Breath congregations. Our experience has taught us that leaders are panicking about numbers that paralyze creativity and innovation. Out of Breath congregations must give up their old picture of success in order to shift behavior. In other words, now that you have identified where you are on this chart, embrace the reality and let go of the guilt. Jesus changed the world with a small group of twelve (plus their wives, of course) and they started house churches of 20-40 people. Tending the Christian movement is less about size and more about discipleship. Being Out of Breath is not a crisis, it is a reality in a changing world. The crisis happens when leaders and congregations wait too long or ignore the reality and keep doing what they have always done. Small changes can make a big difference.

The Leadership Style that defines Out of Breath is "Consensus."

Consensus building is an effective process for conflict resolution. It allows many people to provide input for decision-making which is important for developing trust. As a primary leadership style, however, consensus building has been shown to create mediocrity in congregational life over time. It has also proven to reduce curiosity and learning.

In times of great change it is impossible to build consensus fast enough to allow visionary leaders to cast vision or innovative leaders to experiment. New leaders and growing leaders will find this to be a major frustration.

Moving from consensus building to a purposeful, values-based ministry is a delicate journey that requires trust, conviction of purpose, clarity of core values, and in some cases, baby steps. A congregation will struggle to grow as long as it requires consensus to make decisions.

6 Four Growth Indicators and Stalled Congregations:
Done learning

On a spiritual pilgrimage, there are times when we would rather celebrate the past than look ahead to the future.

By the fourth day on the Inca Trail even though I knew I would reach our destination later in the afternoon, moving forward took all the focus I could muster. Every bone in my body was saying "sit down!" When I finally left my warm tent to join the others, I realized most of the tents were already down and there was new energy in almost everyone except me. Today was the day we would get to Machu Picchu.

It took me a few minutes to realize that my reluctance to move was not just physical; it was emotional and spiritual too. Even though the hike had been grueling at times, I was not ready for it

> The sacred valley can narrow our perspective, driving people to look to the past at what is known rather than looking to a future that is largely unknown.

to be over. There was something so wonderful about being in the Andes that I was sad to see it end. But there was more. The pilgrimage itself had provided me with a huge block of time to reflect and pray. My so-called normal life is not as full of margins for this kind of deeper faith wondering as I would like. I still had things to think about, pray about, and explore in my heart. So I hiked this last leg of the journey alone. I needed each and every step to help ease my transition from the Sacred Valley. I found myself nostalgic about this story and oddly attached to the way of life we had created in only a few days. The interdependence shared between people of different ages, cultures, and lifestyles felt so right that I was clinging to every last moment. It might sound silly but I was literally dragging my feet!

Human beings can build a shrine to almost anything. Even when we say we do this to honor God, most of the time it is really about us. We cannot help but memorialize what has meaning for us; it is what we do. Think about family traditions that have been passed down from generation to generation. We may add our own little twist to them but they are still recognizable as something our parents did.

It is hard for people to give up what has been meaningful to them in order to try new things. We especially see this in the church where we hang on to faith practices that have outlived their usefulness because it is not actually about usefulness. It is good to be honest about this and name our own needs. What is not good is when these needs get in the way of the mission of the church. It is not our church. We may pay for the building and give money for the ministry or volunteer an ocean of time, but at the end of the day it is God's church with God's mission as the priority. Giving in to physical, emotional, or spiritual needs that enshrine the past stalls us for effective Christian leadership.

There are leaders among us who are stalled and no longer learning. At some level, this can happen to any of us when our personal life or ministry becomes overwhelming. However when being stalled becomes a way of life, the whole community is impacted. Just as a leader's positive energy is contagious, so is a leader's apathy.

Stalled leaders show a resistance to change for many different reasons. They may not be aware that they have stalled. Or they may intentionally dig in their heels, firmly believing that the values they hold from a previous era are important or even better than what they see happening around them. Sometimes they are right, however once they dig in their heels and choose the past over the future, people cannot hear them even if what they are saying makes good sense. The very language of stalled says it all. They are no less faithful but the rate of change in the world or circumstances in their lives have caused them to be suspicious of new ideas. The way they are with others may send signals that convey a sense of stuck-ness without even being aware of it.

In *How the Way We Talk Can Change the Way We Work,* Kegan and Lahey ask, "what do you really want and what will you do to keep from getting it." The authors provide an amazing and somewhat complicated argument that describes a process of awareness to move beyond Stalled. In their book, they provide the following set of recognitions that leaders are confronted with:

⊕ Leading inevitably involves trying to affect significant changes.

⊕ It is very hard to bring about significant changes in any human group without changes in individual behaviors.

⊕ It is very hard to sustain significant changes in behavior without significant changes in individuals' underlying meanings that may give rise to their behaviors.

⊕ It is very hard to lead on behalf of other people who want to change their underlying ways of making meaning without considering the possibility that we ourselves must also change.

> Fear is the glue that keeps you stuck. Faith is the solvent that sets you free.
> - *Shannon L. Alder*

It is possible for leaders who are Stalled to move toward a place of growth.

Stalled communities that refuse to listen to those who challenge the status quo are even less likely to change. Transformation takes a commitment from the leader and the congregation to try new behaviors and it usually requires a sense of urgency or crisis to move change forward. Even then it takes time to wake up to the need to put personal preferences aside for the benefit of something bigger. A commitment to growth that includes a willingness to deconstruct default behaviors and to tackle the hard work of constructing new behaviors is essential. Like any major shift in our lives it is not easy—even when we choose the change. Yet we do this every time we lose someone we love to death and have to find a new normal for life without them, or when we go through a divorce, or remarry, or even have our first baby! We can do what we have to do if we have no choice (death) or value the outcome (life). In theological terms, we are talking about moving from Good Friday to Easter Sunday—and it will not be easy. The path from major death or life change is made a little smoother if the four Growth Indicators are taken seriously. People will be more inclined to move beyond Stalled if the culture provides support for taking risks and accountability for everyone.

STALLED LEADERS ARE OFTEN AUTHORITATIVE

The four Growth Indicators provide a framework for this.

Listen – Opening the Heart

We all need to know we are valued, heard, and loved. We want to feel like we and our point of view, even if it is not popular, are validated. A little time spent listening can go a long way. LEAD recommends developing an intentional listening process that includes surveys, focus groups, and one-on-one interviews. This may seem like a lot of effort in smaller congregations where people think they already know others' perspectives. This listening includes a commitment to gathering information but, more importantly, is focused on building trust. Since change happens at the speed of trust, this listening is worth every minute.

Center – Renewing the Soul

God has not left the church even if people have stopped noticing God. In Stalled congregations the language is always more about "I" and "we" rather than the God language we find in Growing or Becoming congregations. Waking up stalled souls takes persistent, even relentless faith practices. Dwelling in the Word, a practice that means reading the same scripture repeatedly over a long period of time may be very helpful. What is not helpful is moving quickly from one faith practice to another

> You don't think your way into a new kind of living. You live your way into a new kind of thinking.
> - Henri J. M. Nouwen

without letting people fully feel the impact of the practice itself.

If the stalled situation is creating a congregational crisis over leadership or finances, this may provide needed momentum for change. The well-known formula for change is:

$$D \times V \times F > R$$

Dissatisfaction with how things are, multiplied by a **Vision** of what is possible, multiplied by **First** concrete steps that can be taken toward the vision must be greater than the **Resistance** to change.

This formula is a confidence builder for people in crisis as it offers a way forward. In addition, people need to feel and acknowledge the current crisis. Kairos moments, the times often during pain and suffering when God feels close enough to touch, can have meaningful results, making way for transformation.

Explore – Shifting the Mind

Faith communities have collective behaviors much like those of individuals. A congregation can actually have a shared "closed" mindset, as outlined in Carol Dweck's book, *Mindset*. The congregation's "way of being" may include a sense of entitlement, an unhelpful feeling of ownership of "their" church, and clear preferences for what they like or dislike. Generally the way the congregation "thinks" is resistant to change.

It can be very challenging for people to move into a growth mindset, but not impossible. This effort is generally a movement from inside the congregation, sparked and supported from leadership outside of the congregation. Someone or a few core leaders must be willing to lead the change. If this person or group has enough social capital with the rest of the congregation and if they have outside support that offers new thinking and creates a path forward, change can happen. The pace of the change needs to be incremental but if it moves too slowly, nothing will ultimately happen. A consultant or coach from the outside is usually needed to help the congregation stay the course over the extended time it will take to capture a new imagination for being church. Outside support can bring new ideas and accountability but will only be helpful if there is an internal leader or better yet, a critical mass with a passion for the future that grows out of their deepening faith in God. We are talking about courageous leadership that is willing to sacrifice long-time friendships for the sake of the future of God's mission in that place. This can be a painful position to be in so the outside encouragement becomes life-giving during the hard work of transformation.

Connect – Building Strength

As we observe others shifting their mindset, some of us may be open to receiving information in a more objective way. The power of the herd can work positively to bring people together along a new path.

Having said this, not everyone can or will move from being stalled. For some of us, our convictions are what they are. People always seek others who share their perspectives so they can stand together as a force to be reckoned with. The direction a congregation will go depends on whose voice and vision is loudest and clearest. If the clearest vision is being articulated by those that are Stalled, the Growing leaders need to define a more concrete, concise, and compelling vision or agree to be Stalled.

There are times when Stalled congregations do grow without an initiating crisis. These usually occur when a beloved long-time member or a young person leads the way. In these instances, the Growing leaders may even work around those who are Stalled to minimize the negative impact.

This does not mean that some of us are valued more than others but it does mean that the voices of those who seek to create conflict or build walls within the community need to be managed. It is imperative to remember and repeat in our own heads: the church does not belong to anyone; the purpose is for God's mission.

To be totally clear here, Stalled leaders may be any age. They may be long-time members or the new, young pastor. Congregations are especially prone to being Stalled if they have not added new members or invited new people into leadership for a long time. The very act of recycling leaders without asking questions about congregational purpose, values, or governance may cause a congregation to stall and signal the end of its lifecycle.

Stalled congregations can move into Becoming through intentional redevelopment, but just adding a missional pastor is not enough. In fact, this can be a recipe for injury to a pastor and cause the congregation to become further entrenched. It is essential for Stalled congregations to move beyond seeing themselves as a destination. They need an outward view and a few small wins. The Tune In process, developing regular faith practices, and cross-cultural pilgrimage are practices that can help overcome the assumptions and unwritten rules of a Stalled congregation. The direction of people who follow Jesus is outward even if the steps they take are small.

The Leadership Style that defines Stalled is "Authoritative."

An authoritative, top-down or hierarchical command-and-control approach by leadership, even pastors, that is void of listening to the congregation and neighborhood will never create space for the shared learning needed in today's world. Authority relies on compliance and is the opposite of innovation and creativity. It may seem to work in a very small congregation where people are tired and welcome anyone who will carry the load, but it will not lead to growth. Authoritative leadership can be valued by people with this experience in their work-place but, to be very clear, it is not an effective transformational leadership style.

Please note, this is different than a staff-centered governance model where key leaders, paid or unpaid, discern God's vision through intentional listening and carry out decision-making on behalf of the mission. The primary difference here is the purpose. Is the purpose for God's mission (always outward, beyond those gathered) or is the purpose to maintain the status quo or to keep certain key people happy?

Governance may be part of the challenge to overcome. This is especially true in Stalled congregations where governance may be larger or more complex than needed or held in the hands of too few people preventing outward growth. The suggestions noted in Chapter 5 can be a helpful place to begin shifting governance. The work of clarifying roles will be more challenging as people reluctantly give up power. This may be as hard for a called pastor as it is for the matriarchs or patriarchs who have seen themselves as the "leaders" of the congregation for an extended period of time. A conversation focused on "who owns the church" becomes crucial if a Stalled congregation is going to have new life.

As discussed, a clear, concrete vision for a different future, a response to intentional listening in the community, or a crisis can all lead to a breakthrough. Without such a change, people with a desire to grow, a passion for following Jesus, or a heart for peace and justice will usually rebel or leave.

There are times when a gentle, trusted pastor can move a congregation beyond this quadrant but it is rare. Most likely a shift will come from a critical mass of people inside the congregation in partnership with outside help. Sadly, in many cases Stalled congregations with authoritative leadership, lay or clergy, will die. Not every leader or congregation can cross the bridge to Becoming or Growing.

When it becomes clear that a congregation does not have a future, ending well is the next big hurdle. People may get bogged down in distributing the church's assets or focused on their grief, shaming or blaming others for the congregation's decline.

The most faithful way to close a congregation is to use the assets to seed new mission. Using existing endowment funds for mission rather than to keep the lights on for a handful of people who are not able to grasp momentum for mission is most helpful. LEAD has worked with congregations where closing the church has actually been the most energizing part of their Christian life. As they consider the many ways their resources might bless others, their own faith is nurtured. Closing congregations have given away their building for another congregation to be birthed, funded outdoor ministry efforts, birthed Campus Ministries, become seed money for new mission starts, and more. These stories of resurrection are a very faithful, hope-filled way a Stalled congregation can become a genuine gift to God's mission in a changing world.

The sacred valley is an invitation to new beginnings, to new and renewed leadership.

7 Four Growth Indicators and Becoming Congregations:
Leading to live

When we are on a spiritual pilgrimage there are times for new beginnings.

Although we didn't hike together, I was Lizzie's adult sponsor. As a high school student entering her senior year, this was Lizzie's fourth trip to Peru with me. I loved sharing these adventures with Lizzie and was so glad her mother agreed she could come on the journey. As a freshman on her first trip, Lizzie had fallen in love with the people of Peru. Her Spanish was better than mine even then, and I could see that the connections she was making were changing her life.

God was up to something in her life through these trips over the years—and in mine too. It turned out that accompanying Lizzie on her pilgrimage was an important part of my own journey because accompaniment is walking together in a solidarity that practices interdependence and mutuality. One of my biggest joys on the trail was to see Lizzie becoming an independent adult right before my eyes. One of the most humbling was to have her as my tent-mate, caring for me when I got sick.

It wasn't just Lizzie or me that I could see growing as we shared the trail. Pastor Jim and his wife, Louise, obviously felt called to accompany the older German couple on our hike. Melissa and Ashley, two young mothers and leaders in the church who met on the trip, forged an authentic friendship that has continued beyond Peru. Shared experiences, especially an adventure that pushes us out of our comfort zone, is one of the best spaces for God to grow leaders of all ages and life experiences.

If I'm honest about this hike, I would have to admit that as the trip leader, I led nothing. The guides, porters, and community provided the real leadership as a network of companions on the journey together. Being the un-leader of a group of people becoming leaders was an amazing and humbling honor.

The system was greater than any one of us, yet it would not have happened without all of us. The quote from Desmond Tutu that hangs on the wall in my house rang in my head: *"My existence is caught up and inextricably bound up with yours... a solitary human being is a contradiction in terms."*

BECOMING LEADERS NETWORK

Then he [Jesus] said to them all, "If any want to become my followers, let them deny themselves and take up their cross daily and follow me." - *Luke 9:23*

Have you ever wondered where leaders in the church come from? It is a question worth pondering. There are a number of predictable paths to leadership. Outdoor ministries, campus ministries, and college campuses are a few of those places. What is often missing from a list of opportunities for leadership formation are youth groups, women's or men's groups, committees, congregational councils, and choirs. Yet that is where people have spent time in our recent history practicing their faith. Notice the difference between the first list and the second. One has to do with people being formed as leaders by practicing leadership outside of the congregation's system and the other has to do with people supporting the congregation's system. Yet there are congregational ministries that are hybrids, effectively combining elements from both outside and inside the congregation to produce leaders.

For over twenty-five years, through all the changes in our world, Camp Hope Day Camp Ministries continues to have one of the strongest track records for growing student leaders when compared to typical congregational youth groups. The number one comment from congregations that host this day camp led by high school and college students serving the neighborhood goes something like this:

We had no idea our youth had so many gifts and such capacity to lead. We thought putting the young people in charge would never work but they are awesome!

Over 50,000 children and youth across the United States and in El Salvador have proven that when adults make space for young people to lead, teach them to teach the stories of our faith, train and mentor them with real skills, and accompany them as they problem solve and learn to work in community, amazing things happen. God uses courageous leaders like the ones who grow through Camp Hope Ministries in ways we will never fully know. LEAD gets emails and Facebook messages from past Camp Hope staff, including many who now bring their own children to camp or who have their own teenagers serving on a camp staff, telling us that what they learned at Camp Hope gave them confidence and capacity for the things they are now doing in their adult lives. Visit camphopeministries.org to learn more.

Sadly many are not active in congregations because they have found the door to church leadership too hard to enter. For example, former staff member Jenny, runs her own real estate company in Denver. Or Jeff, a dad of four, who, with his wife, is a leader in the

> Engage all ages and generations together in growing a deep, bold, consequential faith.

American Diabetes Association. Or Kristen who has her PhD in US History and chooses to teach students history from more than a white majority perspective. Or the countless educators, healthcare workers, etc. who would tell you being on a Camp Hope staff shaped their worldview, God-view, and self-view.

The list is endless, filled with people who learned how to live in a diverse community, how to discover their own power to influence others, and how to tell their own faith story with confidence. None of these things happen without an intentional effort on the part of a few committed leaders. These leaders are making a way for new leaders to practice their gifts in a safe space.

What doesn't work (yet is often seen) is:
⊕ Typical youth groups focused on a menu of fun activities sprinkled with prayer and Bible Study.
⊕ Youth elected to a congregational council or team without a designated mentor.
⊕ Young people sent to retreats or to serve without adults accompanying them to help make meaning out of the experiences and assimilate new learning into daily life.
⊕ Young people given too much responsibility to manage within the context of their busy lives that are filled with school, extra-curricular activities, family, and friends.
⊕ Young people who are only invited to "help" but never asked to make decisions, take responsibility, or practice leadership.
⊕ Young people who are asked to do the stuff at the church that no one else wants to do, like weeding the garden or sharpening pew pencils, without understanding how these things matter.

You get the idea.

By the way, every one of the things listed is true for people of any age.

The congregation can become a leadership development system. This is a huge shift from the way we typically live out our shared congregational life. The goal is to help people move from Stalled or Out of Breath to Becoming.

Becoming leaders come from all age groups.

These leaders may be people who are new to the faith, new to the community, or new to leadership. Some Becoming leaders are people who have been around awhile but due to life changes are now emerging leaders. They may be newly retired with knowledge, resources, and time to give. Or they may be leaders who are *leading to live* out their faith through campus or outdoor ministries, or youth, as already discussed, who are *leading to live* through mentoring;

they may be people in the pew who feel God stirring their hearts. Becoming leaders are energized, curious, questioning the status quo, and they are very often untrained.

When God calls us into leadership, it is both exciting and intimidating. New leaders may find themselves moving away

from their previous peer groups yet not feeling connected to the existing leadership in a community. Intentional mentoring is important for Becoming leaders. Accompanying them into serving in different ways is essential.

Growing congregations are usually ready for new leaders. They may have systems in place for cultivating Becoming leaders with mentors, training, and resources. However, new leaders offer the biggest challenge for Stalled or Out of Breath faith communities. These new leaders ask clarifying questions that may cause defensiveness in others. Their new and innovative ideas may make the congregation feel uncomfortable or even threatened.

People who are Becoming leaders generally will not stay long unless there is room for growth, innovation, and the opportunity to make a difference.

When they are nurtured in faith and serving in their area of passion, they give of their time and talent because they feel connected to the mission rather than out of a sense of duty or obligation.

The future of our congregations depends a great deal on these Becoming leaders because of the lens they bring. They provide a fresh worldview, imagining possibilities others have not considered. It is imperative for the future of the church, not the future of our committees, that congregations welcome new leadership.

The four Growth Indicators are especially important when it comes to welcoming people that are new, Becoming leaders.

Listen – Opening the Heart

Existing leaders who express an openness to new ideas and ways people can make a difference in the community or congregation automatically invite new people into leadership. This posture of listening includes respect for diversity in gender, ethnicity, age, and socioeconomic gifts. It takes a real willingness to learn from new leaders. Asking them questions and listening carefully to different points of view without reacting puts words of respect into action. Acknowledging that there are many right ways to do something gives new leaders space to enter, make mistakes, and discover new ways of leading.

Leadership in a changing world is called to have a new worldview. We can no longer stay in our cultural comfort zones if we want to join in God's mission. In LEAD's *Work Out Guide*, Dr. Kristen Krueger writes:

> Rather than imagining a national "melting pot" with a variety of cultures seamlessly blended together, it is helpful to look back at moments when tensions arose and attempt to understand how Americans adapted. The history of the United States is not actually a story of melting together. Instead it is a constant exchange of cultural conversations. This process is far from seamless, nor is it complete.

Historians understand that this constant tension between past and present shapes the way people understand our current context.

Historical shifts like the time we live in now don't happen overnight. They are part of a slow movement away from one way of life into another until they reach a tipping point where it feels as though things have actually changed in a moment. We are in this place today. Becoming leaders and, even more so, Becoming congregations are tuned into these shifts in a way that the rest of us are still trying to grasp. They are natives in this new world that feels foreign to others. The only way the rest of us can catch up and move to Becoming is to open ourselves up to new ways of thinking and being. This means intentional shifts in what we do, how we think, and what we value. This is not easy but it can be done—and it starts with listening. Those who are native to the new world emerging around us can lead the way. We can seek them out to guide us. The big shift here is that it feels like upside down mentoring where the younger people guide the older folks. When we put our egos aside, this can be a great journey.

Center – Renewing the Soul

Creating multiple paths for people who are

Becoming leaders, especially those of us shifting from one way of being to another later in life, calls for a variety of ways to deepen faith. These may include invitations into small groups, covenant groups, immersion experiences, or retreats.

There are times when we are more open to what the Spirit is doing in our lives, and faith communities can be ready to meet people in those places. Times of crisis due to the death of a loved one, hitting the bottom with an addiction, having a first baby, or moving from 8th grade to high school, and even retirement are all examples of leverage points for waking up to God. In these moments of transition we are open to God's presence and more likely to take on new behaviors that deepen our faith and our relationships with each other. Oddly enough, these transitions build our courage and resiliency for future transitions.

In congregational life it is important for long-time members to resist a "them and us" posture while accompanying Becoming leaders. This kind of polarization reduces the possibilities of transformation for everyone as people become self-conscious and therefore less risk-taking. It also means facing our "isms." We will have to overcome ethnic, socio-economic, and/or generational biases to celebrate God's love for all people. This kind of growth is a move toward wholeness in every sense of the word.

> Be what you are. This is the first step toward becoming better than you are.
> - *Julius Charles Hare*

Explore – Shifting the Mind

Rethinking internal communication, language, use of space, unwritten rules, and governance is needed as we welcome Becoming leaders. Occasionally existing leaders need to get out of the way when a new leader is emerging to give them space to lead. Generally having an open mindset rather than a closed one is required.

Connect – Building Strength

People that are Becoming leaders are especially in need of affirming communities. Their sense of belonging goes a long way toward the courage to lead. The network between established leaders and new leaders in a mentoring model is a great way to usher in future leaders. Connecting new leaders to existing resources and allowing them to connect existing leaders to alternative resources will create a healthy reciprocal balance between the past and the future.

Networking is one of the most helpful growth tools for Becoming leaders if the network expands the leadership beyond their comfort zone. Seeking out new networks with people who are also beginning to grow and who are asking similar questions is crucial to sustaining a Becoming mindset. When people begin to grow in their leadership they may feel isolated as they recognize their thinking differs from those around them. Over time and with intentionality, leaders find others with affinity for the same passions and perspectives. The steps that lead toward creating or finding new networks are exactly what is needed for the Becoming leader to sustain their own growth as they lead others.

Helpful networks, mentors, and coaches include people who share passions but bring new worldviews. Becoming leaders must expand their relationship world to include a wider population of peers based on ethnic, cultural, socioeconomic status, gender identity, and sexual orientation. Without this kind of increasing diversity they will become Out of Breath as the inertia and closed mindsets of those they lead drain their courage. This is especially important if the leader is taking a stand against human rights issues, an expected trajectory of a growing Christian leader, while being part of a closed mindset congregation.

As Becoming leaders search for meaning and places to express their growing faith, they will not be limited to serving in the church. They will network the church with other organizations, institutions, people, and resources as they align their whole lives around following Jesus.

People who are Becoming leaders are beautifully unattached to the typical permission-giving mechanisms and control systems in the congregation. This can work for them or against them depending on how the congregation responds to their efforts. Making space for innovation will keep these leaders growing and engaged.

Congregations that are Becoming have a special place at the table.

Some Becoming congregations are new startups. Others are moving out of crisis or decline and ready for transformation. In both cases, these congregations will likely need financial support and may need it longer than previous generations of new starts. Success will be measured not just by attendance and giving but by the ways and number of people responding to human need in and beyond the congregation. As these congregations are reaching people who are new to congregational life, practices of generosity will take time to nurture.

Becoming congregations may be targeting different ethnic groups, generational groups, socio-economic groups, or have different ways of being church. This requires maturing faith on the part of existing leaders, a willingness to learn, and a true respect for those they are trying to reach. Outside coaching or accompaniment from judicatory leaders or congregational leaders who have successfully made this jump can be very helpful.

Becoming congregations are more likely to take risks and innovate. They will try new technologies and evaluate existing ministry with a critical eye toward anything that does not welcome new people. They are especially good at sincere hospitality and pilot projects. If you visit a Becoming congregation, you will notice an energy and passion for strangers in everything they do, not the cheesy over the top WELCOME! but a heart-felt concern for people and their life stories. Becoming congregations provide a gift to the whole church for stewarding and learning new behaviors.

The Leadership Style that defines Becoming is "Networking."

People who are Becoming leaders are less likely to be locked into established relationships and more likely to reach out and build new connections. They can link ideas, people, organizations, and experiences together in ways we would never have imagined. As already discussed, networking is a way of life as much as it is a leadership style. Becoming leaders live between the questions and the answers—they are always wondering "what if...?" and "why?" Thinking partners as well as other resources like videos, podcasts, books, movies, etc. are all part of the fabric of the network. These leaders take the risk out of risk-taking by doing their homework. They test their best thinking out loud on others with an openness to real feedback. They take critique seriously with a willingness to admit they are wrong.

Becoming leaders use communication differently as they are not limited by the existing systems or part of the gossip loop. Younger leaders are proficient on social media and slow on email. Older Becoming leaders glean their wisdom from the community. If newly retired, they may have more disposable time than other leaders and

a real passion for serving that leads to their own transformation.

This networking way of being can be adopted by anyone. As people move from a top-down, well trained understanding of leadership that is often quite technical to an organic, adaptive style of leadership, networking helps curate resources. There has never been a greater abundance of information at our fingertips than there is today. We are overwhelmed with the endless possibilities of "just Google it." Yet it is within these trusted relational networks that we can find our way to the tools, resources, and thinking partners that will help us most. For leaders who are truly trying to move from Stalled or Out of Breath to Becoming, one great next step is to consider helpful networks or, if necessary, to start one.

Think of networking like the hub of a wheel: while the spokes are coming and going, the hub holds it all together.

8 Follow to Lead:
Living every day as disciples

The Christian pilgrimage is really one day at a time.

At last, I could see the whole Sacred Valley unfolding in front of me with Machu Picchu in the distance. It was breathtaking. Although I had traveled to this amazing Incan Empire by train in the past, it was a new and different perspective to be entering on foot through the Sun Gate. I found myself reflecting not on the trip but on the concept of point of view. I am certain that each of the 22 people on our hike would be sharing a different story if they were writing about their journey because at the end of the day a pilgrimage has a personal element. That does not discount our shared experience. In fact, I think it makes the whole thing richer.

As I hiked this final stretch, I began to feel more relaxed. The path was smooth and the descent was manageable for the first time in days. We were finally at an altitude where I could breathe easily. I actually got out my camera and started taking photos of the beautiful flowers

> And now faith, hope, and love abide, these three; and the greatest of these is love.
> - *1 Corinthians 13:13*

all around me. I turned the corner and BAM! I almost hit the wall.

Right in front of me there literally was a stone wall. I looked around for a minute to see if I had gone the wrong way, but the path clearly ended at the wall. Really? Was this some kind of joke?

As there was no one else in sight, I had to move into problem solving mode. So much for coasting into Machu Picchu!

The wall was almost completely vertical—more so than any ladder or staircase I had ever seen. It was about 10-12 feet high and made of the smallest, narrowest, stone steps possible. The face of the wall was like one of those rock-climbing high-ropes courses I'd done with youth groups over the years. Only there I was safely tethered to a belay!

I waited, but no one was coming behind me. Out of total anger and frustration with the situation, I put one hiking pole on the first step, and then the other and literally climbed up the wall. Right pole, right foot, left pole, left foot. I was holding the poles so tightly that they became extensions of my arms. I did not look down. I leaned into the wall and gritted my teeth as I very, very slowly made my way.

The whole thing probably took about 10 minutes but it felt like an hour. When I got to the top, I literally belly crawled over the lip of the cliff. When I finally stood up with weak knees and racing heart, there was my guide!

Where was he when I needed him as I began the climb?

Oswaldo looked at me and said, "I've never seen anyone climb the wall the way you just did."

Seriously not funny!

Apparently most people, maybe everyone else, bear-climbed the wall. I wondered why I had used the poles. Habit? False security? I also wondered why no one had prepared me for this part of the adventure. Really unfair!

With shaky arms and legs, I made my way to the overlook at the face of the Sun Gate where I watched as Machu Picchu woke up to a new day and shared "wall" stories with the others. Some of our group who had been to Machu Picchu and taken the tour in the past opted to go into Aguas Calientes, a nearby town, for a beer while the rest of us made our way on tired legs around the ruins.

It was at this point that I realized that Oswaldo was not only a fantastic guide on the trail, he was also a great lover of the Sacred Valley. He shared stories with more passion and wisdom than I had ever heard from tour guides on my previous trips. As he described the ancient empire that had inhabited this beautiful place, I wondered what became of them and their way of life, but I was too tired to ask.

Reading my mind, Oswaldo told me about the theories explaining the end of this

civilization. According to many historians, it was due to a combination of circumstances including natural decline, a major outbreak of smallpox, and finally the Spanish Conquerors.

I learned that Machu Picchu was in the center of the Inca Trail which was really a web of trails spanning the Incan Empire that were used to carry supplies with alpacas and llamas and by runners (chasqui) delivering messages.

I also was reminded that on July 24, 1911, Hiram Bingham was led by a Quechua-speaking resident, Melchor Arteaga, to the ruins of Machu Picchu. A year later Bingham led the expedition that excavated Machu Picchu. He became convinced that Machu Picchu was Vilcabamba, the last Incan Capital, and it wasn't until the mid-20th century that his claim was seriously disputed. As I once again listened to the fascinating

history of the Incan Empire, I was struck by two things:
1. No way of life lasts forever.
2. Now I really understood why this is called a "sacred valley."

A valley is a beautiful thing, not just because you might find a treasure like Machu Picchu but because it truly is an open space in the topography of the landscape. It carries more than the literal meaning though because it implies an openness between two ways of life.

What we hold sacred shows in our lives even if we don't realize it. The people who know us, know our values—our sacredness. Once in a while our sacredness spans beyond our life to future generations. I'm praying that what grows out of my life shows the ultimate sacredness of God's love for all people. ¡Buen Camino!

Therefore, since we are justified by faith, we have peace with God through our Lord Jesus Christ, through whom we have obtained access to this grace in which we stand; and we boast in our hope of sharing the glory of God. And not only that, but we also boast in our sufferings, knowing that *suffering produces endurance,* and *endurance produces character,* and *character produces hope,* and *hope does not disappoint us,* because God's love has been poured into our hearts through the Holy Spirit that has been given to us.

- Romans 5:1-5

Nothing happens without leadership. Nothing.

Throughout history, God has used people to get things done. It is our turn. For better or worse, here we are, carrying the mantel of leadership during a time when our world is changing faster than ever before. So what will we do?

This "what will we *do*" question is at the heart of growth, after faith, because it points to behaviors. Behaviors produce something, sometimes good and other times not so good. When behaviors become patterns and patterns become a way of life, we have a system. Systems are bigger than any one person and they are linked to other systems. Think about the eco-system as an example.

Since nothing happens in isolation, the way we behave has influence. Yet systems resist change and new behavior is usually not welcomed. This may sound a little like how your congregation responds when introduced to something new.

In *Accelerate,* John Kotter writes:
> People don't want to reorganize, so they don't think clearly about what is needed or pay attention to competent recommendations from others. They use their conventional process which selects and implements the new global ... system too slowly and expansively. They think current policies and products are just fine

when, in fact, they are not. It is not too difficult to see a part of the problem here. Habits keep us doing what we always do. We resist being pushed in new directions that make no sense to us. We cling tenaciously to what we value and fear might be lost. To behave otherwise is somehow less than human. But there are also less visible forces at play, and in many ways they are much more powerful because they are systemic.

Kotter goes on to say that the only solution to this problem is to create a force powerful enough to reduce and counteract this formidable systemic inclination to stall change. Traditional task forces, teams, strategic plans, programs, and consultants do not come close to creating that force. It requires a sense of urgency. Urgency, in this sense, means that significant numbers of people wake up each morning with a compelling desire in their heads and hearts to do something to move things forward toward a big strategic opportunity.

Kotter calls this action of accelerating around a strategic opportunity the secret sauce. As people of faith, we call this discipleship.

This is not the old membership model of discipleship that grants special decision-making benefits to those who give generously. We are talking about people who seriously think about what Jesus did and try to live it out in their own lives every day.

This is not for just a few key leaders—it is for everyone.

We are talking about a movement here—a get up and get going parade of leaders who are interested in what the Holy Spirit is already cooking up. For this to happen, people need to know what is going on in the congregation, in the community, and in the world. They need to be invited to think seriously together about what these changes mean—for better or worse. There is a greater chance they will get excited by the possibilities for experimenting and being part of this movement when they are involved in the process. We need to be able to answer the question: "Why?"

Early adopters can help everyone listen with open minds by inviting them into the conversation, not creating a "them and us" divide. Research shows that when some people in the group are "in the know" and information is hidden from others, groups easily get polarized.

We all listen best to new thoughts when the information comes to us in multiple ways, especially if it has some emotional pull. Listen is actually one of the four Growth Indicators. The LEAD resource, *Tune In*, provides a step-by-step guide for listening to God through prayer, in the congregation, and in the neighborhood. It is available at waytolead.org/tune-in. Intentional coaching can also help with this process (waytolead.org/coaching). Hearing from many voices rather than a small core group of elected or appointed people on a planning team makes a big difference if our goal is to get a critical mass working on these four Growth Indicators.

This is about building capacity with intentional shifts away from reactivity. The gap between what is going on and what the future looks like gives space for creative tension. This gap can either create space for conflict, if the listening process has not been done well, or it can generate energy like a rubber band stretching between two poles. The energy produced can be used to generate a new future.

Once we are listening, we need to identify what matters most to us. Clarifying purpose and the three different kinds of values (Core Beliefs, Core Convictions, and Core Practices) build confidence for making change. It is a lot easier to make hard decisions once we are centered.

There is an opportunity to revisit assumptions that have held us together in the past. Exploring current governance models, worship patterns (including times), use of space in buildings, the way of being with each other, even staffing all matter if we hope to become a growing, forward-moving congregation. This kind of exploration starts at the top with those in official and unofficial leadership positions and expands like a spiral to include the whole congregation.

Finally, if we are serious about creating a sense of urgency for forward movement, we need to strengthen our connections with each other and our neighborhood. Building a real sense of trust between the leaders and the rest of the congregation is imperative. Of course not everyone will like everyone else, but we are talking about something more than "like." We are talking about connections that are deeply relational and at the same time worthy of respect because they grow out of our core values. They are deep because they are embedded in our

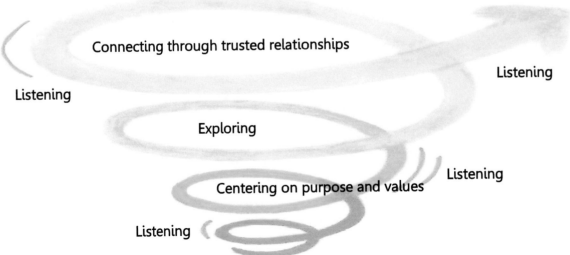

Connecting through trusted relationships

Listening

Listening

Exploring

Listening

Centering on purpose and values

Listening

Understanding the urgency about what's going on in our world & our congregation.

understanding of being a baptizing community. Not everyone has to like everything the leaders do, or even like the leaders themselves, if they can actually see the value the leader is adding to the overall community and can connect this to their baptismal promises. For example, if elders in the congregation do not love changes made in worship life but see that their children, grandchildren, or even faith children they have taught in Sunday School over the years are getting more connected and growing a deeper faith, they will be more likely to have an open mindset. The story needs to be told.

This movement out of a sense of urgency for people of faith is not about instilling panic. The fear-based, manipulative leadership we find in our society is not helpful. We are talking about an urgency that grows from deep listening to God, from leaning into our belief that Christ died, has risen, and calls us to join him in telling the story of God's love and grace in a hurting world.

Our motivation does not come from a fear of death because in the end, death is not our enemy. Our motivation is not about saving a building, cemetery, or even preserving a way of life. We are moved to action out of God's love for us and our desire to make this love known to others. It is only from a position of knowing we are loved that we can let go of our sacred cows in order to join God's movement. Because we believe we are loved, we have no boundaries on loving our neighbor even when that means confronting our own racism or learning about life in a different socio-economic system.

Congregations who are committed to growing can use LEAD's online Congregational Assessment (waytolead.org/assessment) to establish a baseline on the Leadership Landscape for each of the four Growth Indicators. As change is introduced, the Congregational Assessment can be taken again to provide an objective method for evaluating growth.

Our experience has taught us that we can tell a lot about a congregation based on their response to questions that focus on four specific behaviors.

The LEAD Assessment does not ask questions like, "do you like our worship?" It asks twenty questions that focus on how your congregation is responding to the four Growth Indicators. That is: how well is your congregation Listening? Centering? Exploring? Connecting?

In order to obtain meaningful results, LEAD recommends that at least half of the worshiping community take the LEAD Assessment. Encouraging a diverse cross-section of the congregation, based on factors such as age, gender, and ethnicity, to take the Congregational Assessment will offer a better perspective. People do not have to be members to complete the Assessment.

LEAD CONGREGATIONAL ASSESSMENT

Church on the Corner Overall: Becoming

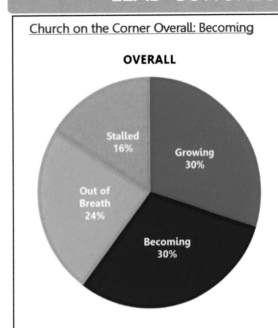

BECOMING Congregations are *leading to live*
- ⊕ Discovering their purpose and values
- ⊕ Learning to be community-centric
- ⊕ Have highly committed leaders
- ⊕ Worship and music may be indigenous to the community
- ⊕ Vision leads finances and staffing, governance is missional

Leadership Style: Networking

Indicators	To grow, Becoming need:
Listen	Deeper understanding of neighborhood
Center	Clear purpose and values
Explore	Financial partners, visionary governance, places for people of all ages to deepen learning
Connect	To expand skills for leaders, build trust, create places for belonging

A sample of a LEAD Congregational Assessment

The Congregational Assessment results include your congregation's results for each of the four Growth Indicators. Once you know where you are on the Leadership Landscape, there are many ways to begin growing your congregation.

Registering for The LEAD Assessment includes access to resources that are helpful for encouraging participation as well as an overview for the Pastor or Council President to complete.

Once the congregation has completed the Assessment (over 3 weeks or less), the leadership will receive a downloadable report from a LEAD coach. The coach will walk the key leaders through the report so that they are ready to share the results with others. The coach's recommendations for next steps are shared without pressure toward a specific path.

These next steps may include heading out on your own congregational pilgrimage using one of LEAD's resources designed to deepen faith. Each of these processes include ten steps and can take from 6 months to a year to accomplish. LEAD does not recommend moving too quickly with the intent merely to check each step off the list. Instead, think of each process as part of a spiritual growth initiative.

To begin, your congregation might:
1. Launch an intentional listening process that focuses on listening to God in scripture and prayer, in the congregation, and in your neighborhood. This is called the Tune In Process. (waytolead.org/tune-in)
2. Clarify your Center by identifying your three types of core values, naming your congregational purpose, and working toward ongoing alignment. This is called

the Wake Up Process. (waytolead.org/wake-up-process)

3. Ask systems questions by exploring your congregation's narrative or theology, looking closely at your governance and staffing, and expanding a culture of generosity. This is called the Dig Down Process. (waytolead.org/dig-down-process)

4. Build on your strengths by moving into more vulnerable, transparent relationships that welcome and invite new people into community, moving beyond your congregation's comfort zone and into more diverse relationships. This is called the Work Out Process. (waytolead.org/workout)

If you look at the four Growth Indicators and feel overwhelmed, we suggest taking them in this order. There is a natural flow with one Indicator influencing the next.

⊕ Listening to God in scripture, your congregation, and your neighborhood **(Listen)** guides you as you clarify your congregation's purpose. **(Center)**

⊕ Clarifying your congregation's purpose will guide you as you make decisions around ministries, staffing, governance, and finances. **(Explore)**

⊕ Creating a permission-giving culture with a clear purpose and vision to grow deeper relationships within the local community expands these relationships to include people that have been overlooked or avoided in the past. **(Connect)**

We know that there are other effective assessments available and are open to working with the tools you may have used or are using. LEAD coaches have the skills and experience to begin working with your congregation wherever you are on your journey.

Congregations in Leadership Transition

LEAD has successfully worked with congregations preparing for their pastor's retirement as part of the legacy of the departing leader. We have also accompanied congregations without pastoral leadership as they move from a conflicted situation to a future vision using LEAD's Congregational Assessment followed by one of LEAD's processes. In this way, the congregation increases its likelihood of calling a new pastor who is aligned with the congregation's identity and mission plan.

LEAD does not focus on extreme conflict management. Our gifts are best used once a critical mass of people in the congregation are ready to move forward in mission. This is not to say that the congregation must be ready to speak with one voice but that LEAD is a better partner in mission when there is a missional spirit stirring up passion for "what's next?" rather than rehashing painful stories. LEAD processes are not helpful to a community with a closed mindset that is focused solely on itself. Our experience has taught us that the best way to move most congregations forward is to create a hopeful vision.

Four Growth Indicators across the Leadership Landscape

This chart presents a way of looking at the four Growth Indicators. There is a fine line between each area and, in fact, congregations that are growing in one of the Growth Indicators may be struggling in another. It is rare to see all four Growth Indicators in the Growing quadrant.

Growth Indicators	Growing	Out of Breath	Stalled	Becoming
Listen	Engaged in the neighborhood, doing justice, deepening relationships	Disconnected from the neighborhood, hosting groups without relationships	Member-centric, little value added to the neighborhood	Neighborhood centered, starting relationships
Center	Aligned around a clear purpose and values, preaching and music are excellent, 50% or more in weekly worship, with many in small groups	Abstract purpose and values, worship and music quality is unpredictable, 35-40% in worship, little involvement in small groups or small groups are cliques	Inward purpose & values, preaching and music are weak, under 20% are in worship, no new small groups or may be resistant to the idea of small groups	Discovering purpose and values, innovative faith practices, preaching and music are improving, worship numbers are fluid, forming diverse small groups
Explore	Finances follow purpose and support staff, governance frees mission, clear invitation for new ideas	Finances lead purpose, staff over-functions, governance is an obstacle, a few people do everything	Finances stop purpose, governance is control with micromanagement and a view to the past	Finances are led by purpose, short on funds, need partnerships, governance is missional, looks to the future
Connect	Purposefully growing leaders of all ages, deepening hospitality, striving to look like their neighborhood	Struggling to engage leaders of any age, little or no leadership development, hospitality is for regular attenders	Recycling leaders, few if any young families with children, think they are friendly but visitors do not stay	Highly committed leaders (often over committed), welcoming of all, working through what it means to be diverse

The big question is "What can we do to grow our congregation?"

Our typical expectation is that to move from where we are to where we want to be as a thriving congregation requires the addition of a NEW THING. We have been taught that growth looks like this:

There are a number of challenges with this way of thinking including a few key facts:

⊕ With this model of change, WE haven't really changed at all. A NEW THING has been added (a staff person, a new building, a strategic plan, a program, a financial investment, a new goal, a training event, etc.) and WE are still doing what we have always done. Sometimes we add new language but the truth is we still do the same thing.

⊕ The NEW THING we add is in ADDITION to everything else. This is a great step toward being Out of Breath as more and more NEW THINGS pile onto the to-do lists of volunteers or staff in leadership.

⊕ The NEW THING is for THEM. We may add something that is great for our youth or our elders or our staff or our you-name-it, but we have not created alignment or harnessed the momentum of the congregation for forward movement. In the worst case scenario, this NEW THING for THEM becomes a THEM and US rather than a new US. It can even unintentionally divide a congregation into factions that create a downward spiral and greater unhealth.

The changes identified in this book are all part of LEAD's focus on healing our congregations from too many NEW THINGS. We are committed to deepening relationships, building trust, and growing in our discipleship. It is possible that there is never a NEW THING or if there is, it grows out of a life of prayer and discernment with leadership that is open to listening, experimenting, and innovating. It looks more like this:

Healing is messy. Taking on new behaviors feels awkward at first. Some people will push back. Others will feel relief and rest a little before engaging as they heal from being over-busy. A Sabbath season is expected as people discover themselves as spiritual beings not merely people who do church. Some long-loved programs will be celebrated and ended. Alignment will move through the congregation with an outward focus. It is good hard work that takes time and commitment with rewards emerging along the way, sometimes incrementally.

A few helpful practices for congregational revitalization using the Four Growth Indicators are outlined in the chart below. "Get it done" type people with black and white checklists will be frustrated at first. They will need to slow down to feel God moving within their own spirit. Movement happens as they personally recover and heal from what can be seen as an addiction to being right, being important, and knowing what to do. This shifts the focus from technical to adaptive leadership. LEAD is skilled at accompanying this pilgrimage. We know this is a little easier when we travel in cohorts as groups of leaders figuring things out together. External accountability from a coach, mentor, or peer network are key to success.

This is one step at a time.

Where will you start?

Growth Indicator (GI)	Stalled? Introducing this GI to leadership, expecting new behaviors	Out of Breath? One group is practicing this GI, influencing the whole	Becoming? Multiple groups are practicing this GI, aligning is becoming a way of life	Growing? Culture is shifting as this GI is fully integrated for expanding mission
Heart... Listen	Interview leaders in your neighborhood or nearby churches	Launch a Listening Team using the Tune In Process	Listen intentionally to local leaders with interest in partnership using Tune in Process	Listen in neighborhood & globally to inform decisions
Soul... Center	Identify the congregation's core values using the Wake Up Process	Identify congregation's purpose and core values using the Wake Up Process	Align all you do around purpose and core values	Use purpose and core values to shape a plan for discipleship and innovation
Mind... Explore	Learn to question assumptions, move toward growth mindset	Staff & council ask hard questions about decision-making using the Dig Down Process	Use clear theological narrative to inform all systems, set and follow through on goals using the Dig Down Process	Create clear metrics, tweak and rethink systems, raise expectations
Strength... Connect	Share personal history and faith stories for relationships with integrity, expand hospitality	Use the Work Out Process to engage hard conversations about race, ethnicity, culture, sexuality & gender	Push comfort zone on issues of human need, expand worldview, focus on integrity of relationships	Create multiple ways to widen worldview, deepen relationships, and increase sincere hospitality

Four stories of congregations on this pilgrimage. What if there was a critical mass focused on the four Growth Indicators?

The stories of congregations that have worked on these four Growth Indicators illustrate how this comes together.

From Stalled to Becoming: St. James Lutheran Church—Santiago Apóstol

For years, St. James was gradually shrinking. Served by a faithful, part-time pastor who was also running a successful full-time accounting business, the congregation was struggling. The neighborhood around them had changed and most of the members had moved away years ago. In time, the part-time pastor decided to retire. The congregation thought seriously about closing—but what would they do with their building? After several conversations with the Bishop's office, listening in the neighborhood, and lots of prayerful discussion, they agreed to redevelop. The new ministry would include an outreach to their neighbors by way of a Spanish language worship service. To do this, they called a bilingual lay pastor.

Today they have a growing Latino congregation with a lay pastor who is studying to be an ordained pastor. They have successfully hosted Camp Hope Day Camp Ministries, empowering their youth as leaders and serving neighborhood children.

But that is not the end of the story! The neighborhood around St. James, or Santiago Apóstol as it is now called by those worshiping there, continues to change. New, larger homes are being built nearby as a diverse, professional community is emerging. Now St. James, with the help of the Bishop's office, has called a Mission Developer to target this population. In less than three years, there are two growing congregations, with two pastors serving side by side as a team. For St. James to catch a new vision, they needed outside partnership, funding partners, new pastors and most importantly, a deeper connection with the community and leaders who were willing to take a chance. The story is still unfolding as these two worshiping communities experiment with adaptive leadership that includes finding ways for two very different socio-economic and cultural communities to be church together. The leaders are committed to taking baby steps forward, doing what it takes to follow God into this exciting and unknown future.

From Growing to Out of Breath to Growing: Kinsmen Lutheran Church

As one of the larger congregations in the Texas-Louisiana Gulf Coast Synod of the ELCA, Kinsmen had a reputation for growing leaders, especially among their youth. This suburban congregation, with the leadership of two new pastors, went through a time of truth-telling where they acknowledged their static faith life and lack of alignment around a common purpose. After hard work with an outside consultant and some ongoing coaching, the congregation's leadership took a few risks. They went through the process of clarifying purpose and values, then the even harder work of organizing and aligning around these new values. They added staff to build on their strength of ministry with children and families. They worked to align their preschool and after school ministry with the congregation's values. The staff would tell you that their work with the outside consultant was a key to developing clarity of purpose, core values, and alignment. Staff took seriously their own personal growth in various ways. Then the senior pastor left.

Kinsmen has just extended a call to a new senior pastor. In the past five years, they have moved from Out of Breath to Growing again. They are positioned to continue as a teaching congregation in the synod. We can look forward to the next season of life as this congregation continues to deepen in faith and expand in mission.

From Out of Breath to Growing: Faith Lutheran Church

Faith Lutheran Church near Houston's Medical Center had been slowly losing steam for years. At one time, this congregation had three pastors. Only six years ago this congregation was polarized with a "them and us" attitude, even within the leadership. After years of trying to move forward in mission with contentious long-time members, the congregation was exhausted. Some long-time members left the congregation. The pastor left and was followed by a long-term interim pastor with skills in conflict resolution. The congregation grew smaller.

Three years ago the congregation called a new pastor. Within a very short time, the pastor had changed the schedule, moved the contemporary worship service into the sanctuary, and helped the congregation clarify its purpose and core values. The core values had been there all along waiting to be named and celebrated. The congregation led a listening process in the neighborhood to validate their hunch that they should call a Latino pastor to the team. Through the process, they were surprised to discover that the nearby elementary school was being targeted as a Mandarin-speaking school. Instead of a Latino pastor, the congregation called a Mandarin-speaking pastor, started a Mandarin worship service, and was shocked to have over 600 people from the community at their first Chinese New Year Celebration. Not only has this congregation called a pastor to serve people who are not there yet, they have added staff to improve the quality of music and administrative excellence and have claimed a focus on healing ministry. They are experiencing growth due to the risks the congregation is taking to deeply connect with the neighborhood, their efforts to bring about alignment, and the strong leadership in the past, during the interim, and today.

From Stalled to Growing: Greenvine Emmanuel Lutheran Church

Located in the beautiful Texas countryside, Greenvine Emmanuel Lutheran Church had been without a pastor for a long time. This small congregation was struggling to stay alive when a pastor moved into the community, not to take the call but to accompany his father-in-law during the last season of his life. Over time, the pastor agreed to serve as interim and eventually as the called pastor of this little congregation. The pastor started a covenant group of leaders who wanted to learn more about following Jesus. After a few years, the pastor led the congregation in a listening process that identified needs within the community for youth and elderly. The needs were more than this congregation could take on. With some effort, the pastor was able to work with other local congregations to form a nonprofit to address the needs of the local community.

Today, Burton Bridge Ministries, a partnership of 12 congregations, is changing

the face of the community. They are not only working with children and elderly but they started a resale store and recently took over the local food pantry. The congregation has almost tripled in size, but the real growth is in their faith life.

Adding your story...

LEAD would love to accompany you in this process. We are very interested in ongoing research as we put these and other practices in place. Please contact us at lead@waytolead.org if you would like to:

⊕ Add your story to our collection of unique places and people God is leading right now

⊕ Have a coach accompany you, guiding you as you live into the four Growth Indicators through a one-on-one coaching relationship or with a cohort of peers

⊕ Learn new practices in your community with the help of a consultant

Rethinking Metrics

9 Measure what matters

All journeys leave an imprint on the heart. Sometimes we have sacred moments when we become aware of the full measure of experience.

A year after walking the Inca Trail, I was sitting on the train with a group making their way to Machu Picchu for the first time. As we got closer and closer with each turn of the track, I was caught off guard with my own emotions. I was almost leaning out the window, unable to stop the tears from filling my eyes or ignore the lump in my throat. Wow—why was I getting so emotional? I could hardly wait to get there. The only way I can describe this is to say it felt like I was going home for the holidays.

I finally got off the train, got the group connected with the tour guide, and disappeared by myself for a holy moment to be reunited with the sacred experience I had found in this place. This might be one of the most intense worship experiences I have ever had. Everything around me spoke of God to me.

Then it hit me that of course I was home. Of course I was worshiping God. Walking here the previous year had helped me find a part of myself that I had not known before. How do you measure this? How do you help someone else understand the things that matter most to you? Typical metrics can't express the spirit of an experience.

By the time I returned to my group, I knew the answer—you tell the story.

Rethinking Metrics
What does your congregation measure?

Congregations typically use metrics like worship attendance and weekly offering to measure their success. While these may help paint a picture of where things are at a particular point in time, they leave out a lot of the story that really matters.

By charting these numbers over time, trends emerge. The trends themselves have an impact on our level of confidence and may even be used to cast future direction. This is a sobering perspective when you consider the global decline in numbers of people and giving within mainline Christianity.

These numbers tell some hard truths. Or better said, they tell a part of the truth. The number of people in attendance is absolutely an indicator of *something* since people vote with their feet. Not showing up for worship or other religious programming is a story worth investigating with genuine curiosity, if there is an openness to use what is learned to transform ministry. Occasionally we will see leaders doing exactly that. More often, though, when numbers of people in worship are declining, leaders are moved to change worship styles without doing any homework to find out why people don't come. Even more troubling is when leaders use these metrics to blame others for the decline. If only our pastor or our organist or our children's programs...

This is not helpful.

Largely these metrics are working against a congregation's vitality and vision of a hopeful future. They cause us to feel hopeless, to fear trying new things at the risk of making things worse, or to move from missional to personality-driven ministry. LEAD believes this is exactly what over-focusing on these traditional congregational metrics will produce. When caring people feel cornered by data that they are taking personally, circling the wagons is a natural response.

Let's face it, there is a lot we cannot control as we lead in this ever-changing world, but we can and should change what we measure. Here is why:

The number of people in worship and the amount of money in the offering plate are both lag metrics.

> Metrics are not a new idea...
> Day by day, as they spent much time together in the temple, they broke bread at home and ate their food with glad and generous hearts, praising God and having the goodwill of all the people. And day by day the Lord added to their number those who were being saved.
> *- Acts 2:46-48*

A lag metric measures something that has already happened by the time you get the data. At this point there is nothing you can do to change the outcome.

With lag metrics, the data is always lagging. For example:

⊕ How many people are in church?
⊕ How much money do they give?

Both of these are lag metrics because by the time you are counting, it is too late to influence the outcome. There is literally nothing you can do to change the number.

Focusing on lag metrics weakens leadership's ability to make change. Lag metrics are discouraging. They make us feel powerless.

Even worse, over-focusing on lag metrics tends to move leaders toward feelings of guilt, low self-worth, and failure. For leaders who thrive on problem solving, lag metrics may move them into overdrive as they franticly up their game imagining success to be a long list of programs that exhaust everyone involved.

For people who are competitive, an over-focus on lag metrics may lead to lying or exaggeration. We regularly hear leaders admit that their numbers of people in worship are inflated. Based on the current paradigm of success, we fully understand their reluctance to share honest data. Many have gotten so good at manipulating numbers, especially around attendance, that they count everyone who shows up to their building on a Sunday (including those in meetings, AA groups, or Scout troops) as part of their worship metric in order to avoid looking bad.

These lag metrics are undermining our integrity or at the least, causing us to lose our confidence and our focus on God's mission. This is a negative accountability that reinforces unhelpful behavior. It's a losing proposition for hard-working volunteers. It is worth saying one more time: *by the time you are recording a lag metric, there is nothing you can do to change the outcome. (Nothing, that is, except lie.)*

Lead metrics on the other hand are predictive and influenceable.

Lead metrics are the indicators leaders strategically set that have the potential to change the lag metric.

For example:

⊕ What is the one thing we are going to do on a Sunday morning to make visitors feel welcome?
⊕ How many times in the course of a year do we equip, inspire, and support people in sharing their faith story?
⊕ How much money and time is given each month by people in worship to reduce human need in our neighborhood?

Lead metrics are incremental indicators, like a formula that reads:

If you do more of X you will see Y result.

We can all relate on a personal level if we think about our own body weight (and overall health). Our scale offers a clear lag metric. Lead metrics for weight control have been identified. We know what they are, right?

What we put in our mouth shows up on our scale. More junk food equals more weight gain. Or think about counting steps with your Fitbit as a lead indicator. More physical activity can also show up on our scale but in a positive way.

When it comes to weight gain/loss, there are other, more subtle lead indicators worth noticing. When we are honest, we can see these as warnings that help us manage pain later. Our clothes may get too tight. Or our face may look rounder in the mirror. Or our over-all energy level may decrease, etc.

If we spend all of our time mad at ourselves for looking bad in a swimsuit, we are missing the opportunity to change the outcome.

We have the power to shift our own behavior to produce different outcomes when we pay attention to the lead metric before we are in big trouble. We may even discover support systems around us to help when we watch our lead metrics. The point is that these lead indicators can change the lag metric because they come early enough for us to change our

behavior—if we are willing to make the change.

Moving Beyond a Reluctance to Use Metrics

People's attitudes about measurements are based on their past experiences. When people have had a negative personal experience with metrics in their work, family, or even at church, they may feel uncomfortable with this idea. The good news is that when people have a positive experience, new attitudes can replace the old ones. By anticipating a positive experience, we are likely to become highly motivated to experiment with new metrics.

Full-on resistance to measuring ministry can grow out of a lack of trust in leadership or a theological understanding that metrics aren't faithful. Both can lead to some people digging in their heels.

Like in any organization, a change in attitude will not happen overnight. It is crucial for every congregation to identify the right metrics for their ministry even if some people are reluctant to. When done correctly, this feedback promotes accountability and increases quality. By selecting the right metrics, they can also increase trust as they provide new insights, positive results, and momentum over time.

A Way Forward Through The Sacred Valley

As you move from conceptual to practical steps for implementing the leadership behaviors outlined in this book, we want you to know that we are here for you. LEAD has developed and will continue to develop resources to accompany congregational leaders. The work of revitalization is a way of life for leaders in this time of great change.

LEAD recognizes that "How To" questions are the most important to answer. We also know that these answers will be unique to the context, location, size of worshiping community, congregational history, and tenure of pastor (or key lay leaders) of each congregation.

The pathways forward using the model we have outlined in this book can be found on our website, waytolead.org/LEAD-process. These resources are available as your guides for moving forward. Yet as already mentioned, it is usually a challenge for leadership to stay the course with a new intervention long enough for it to actually shift the culture without the help of a coach or mentor. Our experience has taught us that there are leaders who can take a resource and make things happen, but most will benefit from a coach or mentor. Synods and congregations across the country are investing in the LEAD Journey which includes working with cohorts of congregations that are also committed to revitalization, attending Learning Seminars, and regular sessions with LEAD's professional coaches.

LEAD's written resources to help you put each of the four Growth Indicators into practice in your own congregation include:

⊕ The Tune In Process—a ten-step guide for listening deeply to God in scripture and prayer, in the congregation, and in the neighborhood

⊕ The Wake Up Process—a ten-step guide for identifying the congregation's three types of core values, clarifying God's purpose, and working toward congregational alignment

⊕ The Dig Down Process—a ten-step guide for evaluating the current systems in place with special focus on thinking theologically, asking significant questions about staffing and governance, and engaging new ways to encourage generosity

⊕ The Work Out Process—a ten-step guide for working out of your relational comfort zones to develop authentic relationships within your congregation, neighborhood, and world with a particular focus on our racism, sexism, genderism, as well as ethnic and cultural biases

⊕ The Annual Roadmap—seven waymarks that lead a council and staff through an annual goal setting process that builds on research-based values for a vital ministry

⊕ Faithful Metrics—a guide for identifying and implementing transformational metrics

⊕ Seasonal Resources—free resources created each Advent and Lent to deepen faith

Leading with Confidence

Deep, bold, consequential leadership requires the willingness to take risks. It takes the courage that comes from hearing God's voice in your life and the confidence found in trusted relationships. In fact, our experience has taught us that trust is the main ingredient Out of Breath or Stalled congregations need to move into Becoming or Growing.

The Sacred Valley is everywhere—not just the official site in the heart of the ancient Incan Empire in Peru. We lead out of the valley every time we experiment within our personal, family, work or congregational life. We do this with confidence not because we are feeling secure, but because we know that

God's people have always taken risks. We can reflect on the heroes of scripture or on the saints in our own past to recognize that leadership always requires letting go of something we know, understand, and find comfort in to go into the unknown, searching for new understandings with a willingness to be uncomfortable.

Just like walking up a fourteener (a mountain over 14,000 ft) unable to breathe or see the top, the good news is that it really is just one step at a time.

It is our constant prayer that you, the reader of this book, find the confidence you need to lead during this time in The Sacred Valley.

Glossary of Terms used in The Sacred Valley

Adaptive change

Problem solving that requires organizations or individuals to do things they have never done before. This means moving off the map to challenge their deeply-held beliefs and values for the purpose of growth. Adaptive change is necessary for true growth and innovation.

Church

A gathering of believers. Church is not limited to a specific space, nor is it defined by the number of people gathered.

Congregation

A community of people working out their faith and life together, gathered with intention to grow deeper in their faith in God, their relationships with each other, and the world around them.

Core Values

Core values are the ideas at the center of an individual or organization's belief system. Once core values are defined, every decision made should align with these values. LEAD understands that congregations have three different kinds of core values operating at the same time. These are Core Beliefs (Biblical, theological perspectives), Core Convictions (priorities for congregational life), and Core Practices (the primary activities of the ministry that align with Core Convictions and Core Beliefs).

Congregational Purpose

The reason a congregation exists. This provides the intention behind a congregation's decisions and actions. Congregational purpose should be shaped by the congregation's core values.

Culture

A collection of knowledge, experiences, values, beliefs, and attitudes shared by a group of people. Culture is at the core of an individual's worldview. It influences language, behaviors, traditions, manners, notions of time, spatial relations, and communication. Culture is a learned experience.

Dig Down

The Dig Down Process is an adventure in thinking theologically, exploring governance and staffing, and maximizing resources. Making shifts in these three important areas can empower a congregation to move forward in mission. An Exploring Team guides this 10-step program designed for deep thinking and action. Each step includes reading, conversation, and discernment toward the larger goal of evaluating and making changes as needed within the congregation.

Disciple

A follower of Christ actively wrestling with the question "how can I live out my faith in the world?"

Diversity

A system that places high value on including voices from a wide variety of perspectives. This includes considering race and ethnicity, gender, sexuality identity and expression, socioeconomic status, age, region, faith, education, and political persuasion. Creating space where a variety of views are not only welcome, but where leaders have actively sought out the perspectives of those not represented.

Ethnicity

An affiliation with a particular group tied to an individual's national or cultural tradition and identity.

Excellence

Deciding that it is not enough to accept the status quo or just "get it done." Excellence demands that leaders work at the highest level possible, even when it is uncomfortable, in order to earn quality results.

Frame

A frame is a lens intentionally applied to a situation to help make decisions. Frames are intentional and often proactive. For example, a person may choose to view a situation through the frame of a specific scripture passage or set of guidelines.

Gender

A social construct that defines the differences between male and female. Social scientists understand gender as a spectrum rather than as two opposite ideals. Gender can be tied to biological sex but often is separate. Gender norms, relationships, and roles are socially driven and vary from culture to culture. Individuals who do not identify with a culture's traditional gender norms may experience stigma or ostracism.

Intersectionality

Intersectional Theory was born out of the Black Feminist Movement, an effort for black women concerned with equity to say that their femaleness and their blackness could not be understood separate and apart from each other. A key component of understanding the intersecting realities that make up our identity is to understand how those realities are viewed within society. Identity is not enough. We as people of faith must dive deeper in our own understanding of how the various forces around us give meaning to identities—good, bad, or indifferent. We are not somehow separate or apart from the systems and influences that govern our lives. Intersectional Theory offers us a way of knowing that can deepen our engagement with our neighbors and within our community.

Lag metrics

Lag metrics measure something that has already happened by the time you get the data. At this point, there is nothing you can do to change the outcome. These indicators are largely output oriented. They are the result of lead metrics when used intentionally.

Lead metrics

Lead metrics are indicators that leaders strategically set, with the potential for changing the lag metric. They are predictive indicators that help shape a path forward. Lead metrics focus on process and define preemptive actions that lead to specific goals. These can be difficult to measure but are a key part of building a strategy for growth, particularly when used in combination with lag metrics.

Leader

Every individual has the ability to be a leader. Leaders exert influence in one or more areas of their life. Leaders may be the most outspoken people in a group but are equally likely to be quiet and thoughtful. Leadership can be taught and leaders are constantly learning.

Leadership Landscape

An ever-changing environment that varies through time. The Leadership Landscape is a circle divided by two axes into four unique quadrants. Leaders of all types and in all stages of life can place themselves and their congregations on the Leadership Landscape.

Metrics

A method of measurement. Metrics assign values to the goals of a project. Every project should have clear goals and outcome expectations that can be measured in some way. By clearly defining the metrics at the outset, it becomes easy to measure the success of a project and to see the ways in which it can be improved.

Mindset

A mindset is not fixed. Individuals and groups can move between a closed mindset, one that does not allow space for change, and a growth mindset from which an organization can thrive.

Neighbor

LEAD calls congregations and individuals to understand their neighbors both locally and globally. This means getting to know the people in your immediate area, those who can walk to your meeting place, as well as holding a constant awareness of the global connectivity of our world.

Pilgrim

A person who embarks on a spiritual journey with the understanding that the process matters more than the destination. A pilgrim believes that the sacred is found everywhere, not exclusively in a church setting, and actively seeks experiences that allow his or her faith to grow as a result of the journey.

Pilgrimage

A pilgrimage is a journey that calls a person to enter into liminal space where he or she expects God to act and expects to be different because of God. If Christians truly believe and live out the resurrection and a theology of God's amazing grace, we can move beyond a faith focused on salvation to a faith grounded in how we live each day. A pilgrimage includes traveling with others, particularly those with diverse views and lifestyles; understanding that all life is sacred; and living in community with a high regard for others encountered along the journey.

Sexuality

Sexuality is the combination of an individual's gender identity, sexual orientation, and gender roles. Individuals may define their own sexuality.

Stakeholders

A person who has invested in an organization, idea, or practice. Stakeholders can help move an organization forward by investing in growth as defined by a leader or they can slow change by rejecting forward movement. A strong leader will work to build support with the organization's stakeholders. If the stakeholders lend support, the community will usually follow.

Technical change

Problem solving with a clear solution that ultimately reinstates the status-quo. Technical change may ask organizations to alter details or goals but do not require challenging fundamental systems or beliefs.

Tune In

The Tune In Process is LEAD's ten-step program undertaken by a congregation to listen to God in scripture and prayer, in the congregation, and out in the neighborhood. A Listening Team guides the process which includes periods of active listening followed by reflection. This process is intended to help congregations connect with their neighborhood through intentional listening.

Wake Up

The Wake Up Process is an effort to more fully align our own lives and our congregation's life with God's mission. A Centering Team guides this ten-step program drawing on ancient Christian prayer practices, faithful discernment, and strategic thinking to clarify congregational core values and purpose in alignment with God's mission. It's about missional identity formation.

Work Out

The Work Out Process is a ten-step program undertaken by a congregation to accompany leaders as they deepen their theological understanding, expand relationships beyond their comfort zones, and recognize the gifts, resources, assets, and humanity of all people. A Connecting Team will lead the process in the congregation by first moving through the steps themselves and then preparing to lead others in small groups through the Work Out Experience.

Worldview

A way of looking at the world that is informed by life experiences. This shapes an individual's reaction to a given situation. For example, a person's childhood, language, country of origin, and travel experience will shape his or her worldview as each experience impacts the way an individual views the world.

Books Referenced

Accelerate. Kotter, John.

Ax.i.om. Hybels, Bill.

Blue Ocean Strategy: How to Create Uncontested Market Space and Make Competition Irrelevant. Kim, W. Chan and Renée Mauborgne.

"The Dawn of System Leadership." Stanford Social Innovation review, Winter 2015, Volume 13, Number 1, 31. Senge, Peter, Hal Hamilton, and John Kania.

Decisive: How to Make Better Choices in Life and Work. Heath, Chip and Dan Heath.

Drive: The Surprising Truth About What Motivates Us. Pink, Daniel.

Evangelical Lutheran Worship. Evangelical Lutheran Church in America.

Generations Together. Amidei, Kathie, Jim Merhaut, and John Roberto.

The Great Emergence: How Christianity is Changing and Why. Tickle, Phyllis.

How the Way We Talk Can Change the Way We Work. Kegan, Robert, and Lisa L. Lahey.

In the Name of Jesus. Nouwen, Henri J.M..

Influencer. Patterson, Kerry, J. Grenny, D. Maxfield, R. McMillan, A. Switzler.

Inside the Large Congregation. Beaumont, Susan.

The Leadership Challenge: How to Make Extraordinary Things Happen in Organizations. Kouzes, James M., and Barry Z. Posner.

"Making Dumb Groups Smarter." Sunstein, Cass and Reid Hastie.

Mindset. Carol Dweck.

NurtureShock: New Thinking About Children. Bronson, Po and Ashley Merryman.

The Practice of Adaptive Leadership. Heifetz, Ronald, Alexander Grashow, and Marty Linsky.

Switch: How to Change Things When Change is Hard. Heath, Chip and Dan Heath.

"Tune In to God calling people of faith into the neighborhood & world," Living Every Day As Disciples.

"What is A. A.?", *Alcoholics Anonymous World Services, Inc.,* Accessed January 2015. http://www.aa.org/pages/en_US/what-is-aa

The Wisdom of Desmond Tutu. Battle, Michael.

Gratitude

No one writes a book alone. We actually do not do anything alone. God is ahead of us leading the way and gifting our lives with people to accompany us: leaders. Thank God.

My name on the book is a symbol of the amazing people across the world who have shaped my thinking, the wonderful books I have read, the love and support I have received from my family (who share my values and understand my call), and the teams of highly committed, gifted, and passionate people I have had the privilege of experimenting with. I especially want to thank my husband, Dewayne Hahn, and my children, Justin and Catherine, Kristen and Karl, Patrick and Kelli, Jeff and Danielle, and Matt, whose love give me courage to lead.

This book is a work of the heart by a few people who are on this pilgrimage with me—the LEAD Team. It is the sum of our best thinking. These people include my core partners, Chris Hicks and Beth Hartfiel, who have edited and offered their amazing perspectives. When I agreed to update this book, the entire LEAD team stepped up to be part of the adventure for which I am deeply grateful.

This book is also a prayer. A real, sincere prayer that it moves you, the reader, to hear God's call and to respond by listening, centering, exploring, and connecting.
¡Buen Camino!

Peggy Hahn

Additional books in the series:

Tune In: Calling people of faith into the neighborhood & world

Wake Up: Calling people of faith into God's mission

Dig Down: Calling people of faith into a growth mindset

Work Out: Calling people of faith into meaningful relationships

Faithful Metrics

Peggy Hahn is a passionate champion for growing leaders and dreams of faith communities attracting people of all ages and cultures as they make a difference in their neighborhood and in the world. She has served three congregations in two states and as Assistant to the Bishop in the ELCA Texas-Louisiana Gulf Coast Synod for more than 33 years. Peggy is the Executive Director of LEAD, a non-profit focused on resourcing and coaching church leaders who want to make adaptive changes. Peggy received the 2014 Tom Hunstad award and has served the ELCA Youth Ministry Network as a coach to the board, a workshop leader, and intensive care course teacher. She has coordinated service project for 36,000 people at the 2009 and 2012 ELCA Youth Gatherings in new Orleans and was the innovator of Camp Hope Day Camp Ministries and the Disciple Project.

Peggy has made her enthusiasm for the gospel known in the U.S. and around the globe. She has led groups to Spanish-speaking countries for more than 20 years and is still trying to learn the language. She has survived being hit by a motorcycle in Africa, has hiked the Inca Trail, and has eaten *papoosas* with dear friends in El Salvador for 25 years.

Peggy is married to Dewayne Hahn, lives in Houston, hangs out in the country in Smithville on weekends off and calls New Orleans home. She loves to garden, read, walk, and any time she gets to spend with their five children and six grandchildren.

Made in the USA
Lexington, KY
14 January 2018